CONTENTS

Chapter One   *4-49*
THE CONQUEROR

Chapter Two   *51-93*
   THE SPIRITUAL COVER

Chapter Three   *95-166*
THE SIGNATURE OF THE FATHER GOD

Chapter Four   *170-206*
   INSPIRATIONAL WRITERS

Chapter One

THE CONQUEROR
THE SPIRITUAL COVER
THE SIGNATURE

Conqueror, Cover and The signature

KING SOLOMON SPIRITUAL LIBRARY THE GOD ENCYCLOPAEDIA WORD OF INFINITY

**BY
THE SPIRIT OF THE FATHER GOD
THROUGH HIS SERVANT
HRM KING SOLOMON DAVID
JESSE ETE**
(King Solomon Spiritual Library)
Eteroyal Universal Family - BCS

All rights reserved
Copyright © Solomon ETE, 2008
Solomon ETE is hereby identified as author of this work in accordance with Section 77 of the Copyright, Designs and Patents Act 1988

The book cover picture is copyright to Solomon ETE

This book is published by
King Solomon Spiritual Library
P O BOX 27394
London E12 6WW UK
www.kingsolomonspirituallibrary.com

This book is sold subject to the conditions that it shall not, by way of trade or otherwise, be lent, resold, hired out or otherwise circulated without the author's or publisher's prior consent in any form of binding or cover other than that in which it is published and without a similar condition including this condition being imposed on the subsequent purchaser.

A CIP record for this book is available from the British Library
ISBN 978-0-9559801-9-0

FATHER'S TALK
(GOD PRESENT)

Christ Our Lord, Twenty-third Simon Canaanite, FATHER, Two Thousand and Eight (BC/OB/BOOH) Saturday, Twenty-third February, Year Two Thousand and Eight (23/02/2008)

In the Name of Our Lord Jesus Christ
In the Blood of Our Lord Jesus Christ
Now and forever more

THE CONQUEROR

THE FATHER GOD IS THE AUTHOR OF EVERYTHING

Today, it pleases **ME, THE FATHER GOD THE CREATOR OF THE UNIVERSE** to give this Lecture Revelation titled: **THE CONQUEROR**.

INTRODUCTION: **THE CONQUEROR IS THE FATHER GOD ALMIGHTY**.

Conqueror, Cover and The signature

THE FATHER GOD is the author of everything. **I** want to make all human beings including human-Gods, human-animals, human-birds, human-fishes and whatsoever type of human being you are, to know that **THE FATHER GOD** is **ALL** and **ALL**.

I want you to use this Lecture Revelation as your very own cover ticket to strengthen your faith in **THE FATHER GOD**.

All positive children of **GOD** must not quit and should not despair in adversity.

Do not quit in life.

Do not worry about the difficulties you encounter in life.

Do not join negativism because of that or anything else. Do not please your negative self because you are afraid.

Do not be afraid.

I, THE FATHER GOD, AM THE CONQUEROR, the victor in everything. **I AM** always victorious.

If you have never believed the **WORD** of **GOD** and if you have never believed information about **HIM**, you must now. Do not wait for vision and prophecy. This is not the time for vision and prophesies, but the time for face-to-face talk. As you are hearing this Lecture Revelation, it is not a matter of vision or prophesies anymore or that you are going to see somebody for consultation, and to see vision for you. This is **The WORD** and **the WORD** is **GOD**. This is **The WORD** that when you listen to, accept and take it in, it manifests instantly according to your heart, what you believe, your acceptance, and what you take in.

THE **WORD** IS EVERYTHING but humanity could not grasp this understanding before now. However, this is **GOD'S** time, which is the best time that the whole world should come into this knowledge about **THE SPOKEN WORD** in that, it is **The WORD** that does everything.

Show **ME** any president, King or Queen, the Police, the Army, Churches etcetera that **The WORD** cannot order. All orders, instructions, protocols and so on are **The WORD**.

What makes people sleep in one place the whole night? What makes people go to a particular place and start dancing like mad? What makes people congregate for one thing or the other? All sorts of activities go on every blessed day in the whole universe.

People move up and down and do all sorts of things. In television, radio and what have you, you see people doing diverse things all over the place. What is it that manipulates all these people? What is the manager of the cacophony of activities everywhere? What makes people all over the world and in all aspects of life behave as they do? It is **The WORD**. So, if you come to this understanding that there is such a phenomenon and such a powerful entity why don't you believe in **HIM** now and be free. Believe that if you sign up and be together with this power - with this **WORD** and this

WORD recognizes you in person and lives in you and you worship **HIM**, your problems are over. Give honour to **HIM** and to this **WORD** then you have no problems again.

Why should people deceive you saying thus?

Oh come I want to give you talisman.

Oh, come I want to give you a ring.

Oh, come I want to initiate you in a secret society.

Oh, come I want to put you in witchcraft.

Oh come to sort out your bad dreams.

Oh, come for this or for that when **The WORD** manipulates all of them. All are **The WORD'S** objects. Anything that **The WORD** has not formulated does not exist.

I AM THE ONLY EXISTING THING! **I AM the Unheard-Able, Unseen-Able and Untouchable** but since those states do not change and were of no benefit to **ME, THE FATHER GOD, I** made **MYSELF**

heard-able from the thought and that is **The WORD**.

What do you do with the thoughts if you do not manifest **The WORD**? What do you do with **The WORD** if you do not manifest action? So, this is the time for action. It is not only the time to just think and hear. It is the time to hear, think and put it into action. So, today, **I, THE FATHER GOD** have come with this Lecture Revelation called **THE CONQUEROR**.

A: **NO OTHER POWER EXISTS**

Do not think there is some other power anywhere else. For those of you who have bits of negative powers and would spend money and dream dreams and would say, let me go and see who is talking like this when you hear this, **I** ask you, how many heads do you have? Tell **ME**! How many heads do you have to go and see who, is talking? Okay, for you thinking like that, what is thinking in you? Is it not **The WORD**? What made you to have that thought as who is talking? Where is that person? It is **The WORD** that is talking. That is **The WORD** that you serve but you are serving **The WORD** in a negative way.

Show **ME** anybody that made a ring with a piece of gold or silver as talisman without adding the words of what that ring would do and expect someone to take it.

Show **ME** anyone that builds a church or puts up any type of building and would not give information on what the house is for and instructions to use where it is necessary and yet people would go there?

Show **ME** anyone that has a child and would not give a name to that child. If you do not name your child, the child would be referred to as a 'thing'. The first thing people do as regards to conception is to give the newborn baby a name. In some cases, the baby is named before birth. That means you have identified **The WORD** that has come to live in the world and that means that there is no other power that exists.

I AM revealing the secret things about **GOD**, which have never been privy to anyone. You only know as stated in the bible that:–

*In the beginning was **the Word** and **the Word** was with **GOD** and **the Word** was **GOD**...*

But how many people believe that or understand those words or are serious about them?

Now, **I** want total seriousness about how to recognize **THE CREATOR OF THE UNIVERSE**, the **ONE** you have been toying about with all this time.

Since you now believe this, you surely need to stand by it. Speak **THE WORD!** Believe **THE WORD!** With that, before anybody brings a knife to harm you, you already have a spiritual knife. Before anybody would load a gun to shoot you, you have already spoken the Word. Before someone goes to engineer something physically for instance, going through all the processes to board a plane to take-off, you have already taken-off.

The **WORD** is aeroplane. While people have the physical one you have the spiritual one. The **WORD** is bullet. While people struggle to put bullets in their gun, your spiritual one is already loaded. The **WORD** is everything.

Will you say tomorrow that you will use this book from KING SOLOMON SPIRITUAL LIBRARY to form another secret society? Because that is, what people do. Now you won't believe all these things but when evil people go and turn things upside down and call them Seven Books of Moses, Seven Secret Solomon this or that, you rush for them. It won't happen like that again oh. This time around there is no secrets. This is an **OPEN SECRET** as the **OPEN WORD OF GOD**!

What is the spirit that brought all those Books of Moses and all the rest of them? **I** have withdrawn all those things. As **I, THE FATHER GOD** has manifested on earth physically and since **THE FATHER'S TALK** (**GOD PRESENT**) has now come, **I** have withdrawn the powers from all those things. This is new and you know that when a new thing comes, the old one is void. **I** have now replaced all of them with **THE FATHER'S TALK (GOD PRESENT)**.

THE EVERLASTING GOSPEL and **THE TESTIMONY OF EVERLASTING GOSPEL** is **THE FATHER'S TALK (GOD PRESENT)**.

I REPLACE ALL THE SEVEN BOOKS OF MOSES AND ALL MAGIC BOOKS VIA **THIS WORD**.

Those are secret and coded words that they use to perform magic and ask people to tell lies. The sharpness of the hand deceives the eye. **I** ban all that! So, do not let any dream worry you again. SPEAK **THE WORD**! **The WORD** forms the dream.

If you see people cover themselves in black or have twenty heads and call themselves witches and wizards and are flying up and down, do not be afraid because it is rubbish. They are objects of frustrated souls as homeless souls. **I** will reveal this to you. There is a Lecture Revelation that **I** will give about '**Homeless Souls.**'

People who call themselves witches and wizards operate through ghosts that have no homes and no place to stay. They use them up and down. Those are homeless souls and they call them witches and wizards. They are frustrated spirits that were disobedient. They can be likened to products of all the stubborn children that run about because of leaving home and so roam about and sleep on the streets. Inclusive are those their wives drove out of their home and those their husbands drove away from their home. This is what evil people are like when the die and form evil spirits.

The evil people and all the frustrated people form all these evil spirits that are everywhere when they die. When you make a little sacrifice that is giving them food they follow you and become available for your use. It is like when you cook food and give to people sleeping on the road as the homeless, they eat without care on how the food is prepared or what is inside the food because they do not care. All they know is that they are hungry and so would just eat whatever food is given to them.

In the same token, when anybody makes a little sacrifice or pay alittle attention to frustrated souls, they serve the person because they have no place to stay. Do you want to be like that?

As you join evil and as you join witchcraft to protect yourself you have lost your life and become homeless as a useless soul, carrying out all sorts of wickedness on people. **I** will catch all of you and put you in the wastebasket burning with fire. Therefore, know that no other power exist except **THE FATHER GOD ALMIGHTY THE CREATOR OF THE UNIVERSE**.

B: EVERYTHING MUST BOW TO THE FATHER GOD.

Everything must bow to **THE FATHER GOD**.

Everything must bow to **GOD THE FATHER**.

Everything must bow to **THE SUPREME WORD**.

If you don't bow physically while you are alive, you will bow when you die. And **I** mean it!

Think well about this information.

Think well about what you are hearing now.

Think well about the new thing that has now surfaced now on earth.

The year Two Thousand and Seven was **MY** victorious year, VICTORY YEAR OF THE LORD. Two Thousand and Six was the end year for the dragon and **I** conquered dragon and **I** established **MYSELF** in the new century EVERYWHERE HERE AND THERE forever and for eternity. So, in Two Thousand and Seven, **I** launched

THE FATHER'S TALK (GOD PRESENT) properly.

Two Thousand and Eight is the beginning of the New World ERA. So, we will start to celebrate. The First Ten-day Celebration of **THE SUPREME WORD** SEASON CELEBRATION was Two Thousand and Seven by HRM Solomon David Jesse **ETE** with **ETE** Royal Universal Family, which was the VICTORY YEAR OF THE LORD. And now the GLORIOUS YEAR OF THE LORD is the year two thousand and eight. Two Thousand and Eight is the beginning of the **GLORIOUS YEAR OF THE FATHER GOD** for eternity.

All those who practice evil, all those who represent Satan, demon and all negativism should know that **THE FATHER GOD** has conquered all evil in the spiritual world. And now, all evil are dying and melting away one by one physically.

C: **THE FATHER GOD RULES ALL PLANETS FOR ETERNITY**

This is not something that will change. You better join the positive side of **THE FATHER GOD**. You better join the positive thing, which includes organizations, groups and so on. If you hear, of an organization, that mentions the name of **GOD**, do not jump in and join. First check the fruits of their operations. Do not depend on hearsay. Find out things for yourself. Check well whether they operate under the truth that is, under the HOLY SPIRIT OF TRUTH.

Look out for any such places that there is no talisman.

They don't believe in talisman
They don't believe in rings
They do not believe in incantation,
They do not believe in idol worshipping;
They are fruitarians and vegetarians –
They only eat fruits and vegetables,
They do not eat meat and fish,

Conqueror, Cover and The signature

They do not believe in killing any life;

They believe in equality, love, patience, humility, kindness and mercy and are charitable. Check well about any such places whether they speak positive words but do not look at the individuals there, because Satan can manipulate individuals. When you see the principles, the norms, codes and conducts of such a place are truthful and they operate under truth and are positive, then know that **THE FATHER GOD** has established there.

Believe in Brotherhood. All Organizations, all tribes, all religions are one from **THE FATHER GOD**. When you read the Lecture Revelation titled ***IN-BETWEEN THE FATHER AND THE SON, THERE IS A SERVANT***, you will come across where **I** revealed what happened between the Muslims and the Christians. **I** also revealed that King Solomon **ETE** is the Servant that will bring them together.

In His Father's House, **THE FATHER** has Abraham. So now Abraham is back on earth. Adam is back on earth and he was Abraham and was also David. They were the same natural Fathers. So everybody must return to that first love. If you don't do that you are in trouble, because all power in Heaven and on Earth is given to HIM to now manage the whole world in peace and love.

Love is the answer. So everything –
must bow to love
must bow to the Spoken **WORD**,
must bow to peace,
must bow to joy,
must bow to oneness, mercy, kindness and righteousness. Think well, speak well, hear well and do well. That is what everybody should bow to now. **THE FATHER GOD** rules forever. That is it!

D: **THINK WELL, IS THERE ANY OTHER POWER?**

Think well is there any other power? It is a question. If you follow **MY** expatiation and what **I, THE FATHER GOD** says step by step, you would know that there is no other power. **I** will give a Lecture Revelation titled *THE BIG QUESTION*

Now, since you know that nobody has the right and no other power has access to you then **THE FATHER GOD** is **THE CONQUEROR**. How will **THE FATHER GOD** be the **CONQUEROR** for you? **HE CONQUERS** through your mind. In spirit **THE FATHER GOD** has already conquered and established the New World – **PEACE.** It is not the new world order of evil. This is THE NEW WORLD PEACE from **THE FATHER GOD ALMIGHTY THE CREATOR OF THE UNIVERSE** managed by **THE SUPREME WORD SPIRITUALLY**.

Do not worry because no evil program will work in this world. None will work. It has never worked and it will not work now! They are only wasting their time. It is the same people that reincarnated to continue with their old evil programs. **I** have thwarted them. Nothing evil will work. Those who do not fear **GOD** will not be afraid of anything.

Do you think King Nebuchadnezzar has not reincarnated? This is the last seventh generation that all negative souls will never be born on this earth again, because they have finished their seven incarnations.

Since King Solomon has come back as Abel, everything has gone to renewal FROM SOURCE TO DESTINATION AND FROM DESTINATION TO SOURCE. His Father Adam is here, THE KING OF KINGS AND THE LORD OF LORDS. King Solomon as Abel is here, so all is well.

Therefore, think well, is there any other power in this world? The answer is - NO! You must say - NO, there is no other power. If you say yes, you will be arrested by **MY ARCHANGEL**

MICHAEL and his group of Angels. You will be arrested immediately. If you say, there is any other power apart from **THE CREATOR OF THE UNIVERSE – THE SUPREME WORD OF THE UNIVERSE – THE CREATOR – THE FATHER GOD** that created everything and if you say yes to this question, you will be arrested immediately in your conscience. As you are arrested in your conscience, you are arrested in the soul, the spirit and the physical. You will be tormented by that evil in you. If you say no – capital NO, then you are free forever.

NO OTHER POWER EXISTS IN THE WHOLE UNIVERSE. In Heaven and on earth it is only **THE FATHER GOD** that exists.

From today use, this Lecture Revelation titled **THE CONQUEROR** as your backing power, backing energy, safety key holder for your life because there is potency inside this Lecture Revelation.

Conqueror, Cover and The signature

I have INJECTED **THE SUPREME POWER POTENCY** INSIDE THIS LECTURE REVELATION just as every of **THE FATHER'S TALK (GOD PRESENT)** is with **POWER**.

When you like and love **THE FATHER'S TALK (GOD PRESENT)** and you love **THE FATHER GOD** then all is well with you. How do you love somebody? You love somebody or you are interested in somebody through the fruits they bear and the words they say. Those things attract you. So, the information in **THE FATHER'S TALK (GOD PRESENT)** is **TRUTHFUL INFORMATION**. If these Revelation Lectures attract you then love it to your soul and you are free.

If in answer to this question: *THINK WELL, IS THERE ANY OTHER POWER APART FROM* **THE FATHER GOD, THE CREATOR OF THE UNIVERSE?** *<u>You say capital NO</u>*! That means you are free from evil. From that day no demon, no witchcraft, no tribulation will disturb you. No matter how many times they plan evil against you, it will boomerang to them, because no other thing gets close to you apart from the Holy Spirit, apart from the positive spirit of **GOD**.

That is the question that is meant for all human beings both positive and negative ones to answer. That also is the goal between you and **ME THE FATHER GOD**. For you to conquer you must answer that question. **I** have conquered and given victory to the whole world that is, to all **THE FATHER'S** positive children, but it is left for you to sign it up today.

The title of this **Lecture Revelation** is '***THE CONQUEROR***'. **CONQUER**! Sign for it! Sign for it! If you sign up for it then you have conquered in spirit and in soul and the physical and otherwise, now and forever more, Amen.

E: **THE FATHER GOD OWNS EVERYTHING**

I AM THE FATHER GOD and **I** own everything, but **I AM** not using force to fight for what **I** own. **I THE FATHER GOD** owns every living thing and **I THE FATHER GOD** gives freewill energy for you to live and accept THIS SUPREME WORD OF **THE FATHER GOD ALMIGHTY**.

What obtains is that, when a family is together, the husband and wife bring up the children together under the same umbrella and with the same directives. In such an ideal situation, the children would not be confused. However, when the husband and the wife are separated the family is thrown into confusion. Children would have to make personal decisions on which of the parents to attach to.

You know that the first GOD THE FATHER and Mother on earth are Adam and Eve, and they were one as a whole. But Lucifer came and separated Adam from Eve by injecting something into them. Since then husbands and wives always quarrel. They always have misunderstanding. When they have children, some copy their father and others copy their mother. Unless couples accept this **FATHER'S TALK (GOD PRESENT), THE SUPREME WORD** for the Holy Spirit to bring them together back in one SUPREME NATURE OF LOVE, many families will continue to be in disarray because of that evil virus in them. This is the meaning of **The Tree of Life, THE SUPREME WORD PERSONIFIED, THE HOLY SPIRIT OF TRUTH**.

Three of Life means all men and women should come back together in unity with **THE FATHER GOD** and in oneness of positive love, before any union as husband and wife. However, if the spirits in them is different then they will have problems. Do you see any peace in marriages these days? So many marriages are pretending marriages and the children that ensue from such relationship are 'wonderful' because they are not stable. They are products from two different spirits.

Nonetheless, this is a golden opportunity for you to believe that **THE FATHER GOD** owns everything and when the mother says yes to the father all becomes well for eternity.

To accept the positivism of **GOD** and be with **GOD** and stand on the positive side of **GOD**, sign on for **THE CONQUER POWER OF THE FATHER GOD, THE SPOKEN WORD, THE ONLY ENTITY, THE SUPREME WORD OF THE UNIVERSE, THE HOLY SPIRIT OF TRUTH, THE FATHER GOD.** You also believe that one man is every man on this earth who is Adam and that one man is also a woman. So, there are no two human beings. **I** created Eve from Adam. In the light of this knowledge, you should now understand that there is only man because he is every man and he is every woman too.

Therefore, stop fighting, stop quarrelling, and stop behaving funny with each other, because when you do that you fight against your life and you will not win. Nonetheless, for those who love **THE FATHER GOD**, **HE** has won for them.

F: **THE FATHER GOD IS THE OWNER OF EVERYTHING BROTHERHOOD**

The meaning of Brotherhood is, THE FAMILY OF THE SAME PARENT – BROTHERHOOD. Every creation, living organisms, living creatures and all that you, man creates put together are the property of Brotherhood. They all belong to **GOD THE FATHER** on Earth and all belong to **THE FATHER GOD** in Heaven and managed by **THE SUPREME WORD** of the universe, **THE CHRIST OF GOD**. Therefore, everything is Brotherhood.

G: **THE SUPREME WORD MANAGES EVERYTHING, HE IS THE INSPIRATIONAL HEAD**

THE FATHER GOD is the inspirational head of, **The WORD** as THE SPIRIT. The Supreme **WORD** is the ONE that takes care of everything because HE is the Converting Machine. HE is the Creator. What you think in your heart can never come to light without you speaking or writing that is, putting your thoughts into words. Putting your thoughts into words is not only by speaking but also through writing. Another means is that you can use your fingers or through sign language if you are dumb to verbalize your thoughts. If you use sign language, it is **The WORD**. If you use your eyes and your eyeballs to put your thoughts into words, it is **The WORD**. If you write with your hands, it is **The WORD**. **The WORD** is the Supreme Manager of all **THE FATHER GOD'S** offices. And that is what **I** call The Christ Office for the **KING OF KINGS AND THE LORD OF LORDS**.

Therefore, this conquering energy, this power, this infusion energy that **I** give to mankind does not need too much talk. Nonetheless, it is not just the talking, but also the power that dwells in the talk, in the wisdom and the understanding according to how you believe. Use your conscience as the Higherself.

All **THE FATHER'S TALK** makes you high and makes you understand how to deal with **GOD** directly because it is a direct word. There is no *corner-corner* and no diversion. It is a straightforward business. It is open teaching. It is the case study of **GOD**. When you do this, you've taken evolution to a Higherself and you have become a more rearranged human being that will work for **THE FATHER GOD** and enjoy your life forever.

CONCLUSION A: **ALL PRINCIPALITIES MUST OBEY GOD**

All principalities must obey **GOD**. It is a must! If you do not obey **THE FATHER GOD**, you are finished because you are a frustrated and a homeless soul.

I, THE FATHER GOD already control all principalities, because there is no way they can exist without **THE FATHER GOD**. What do you use to invoke evil? It is **The Word**. You write some words and speak in the spiritual language and invoke. That 3has now been upturned.

Now, you must speak that same word and;

you must invoke love,
you must invoke peace,
you must invoke mercy,
you must invoke righteousness,
you must invoke oneness,
you must invoke patience
you must invoke positive life of
GOD, the power of the Holy Spirit of Truth.

Those are the powers you have. When you have the spirit of love, you are so powerful and nobody can do anything evil to you. When you have spirit of mercy, you are powerful. The more of the Virtues of **GOD** you have the more powerful you are.

Each of the virtue of **GOD** is a subject and is power.

The twelve positive fruits of Holy Spirit of **GOD** are the twelve powers that are assigned for man in the Christhood Office. That also is the twelve months of the year manipulated by the Seven Spirits of God from which you are born. Everybody must always put to birth in any one of the days of the week. You cannot be born on all the seven days. You must be born in any one of the days of the seven days of the week in that month. So you represent that power.

The reason people do not see the glory of **THE FATHER GOD** is because they do not know these things. Nobody thought them. Some of these people called Astrologers and all other similar ones try to manipulate the idea for themselves. They initiate people and make money out of them. **I** thwart all that.

Today, you have the opportunity to develop yourself to become higherself. Read the Lecture Revelation titled called **'Procreation and Birth'** you will see that **I** have revealed so many things connected to birth. There is information on before a child is born and after a child is born and every other thing is there. Those are the Revelation Lectures that you must use to control birth because they are the powers.

Love is one power
Peace is one power
Mercy is another power
Patience is another power
Oneness is another power
Cooperation is another power
Joy is another power

Everything that is good has power and they are positive powers.

If you hate that is an evil power. If you do all sorts of things that are negative, those are the negative powers that people 'cast and bound.' **I** have sent so many spirit angels to say – 'I cast and ban you. I drive you away in the name of our Lord Jesus Christ. I drive you away!'

Evil is the most frustrated and suffering of all things. They are frustrated homeless spirits souls that are frustrating about everywhere! When you go there a small child would get up and say, 'I ban you away from here.' If you go to somewhere else a woman commands you. Evil never respected women, but now a woman would get up and say to evil, 'I cast and ban you in the name of Jesus Christ!' Tell **ME** how you would want to be like that. When you practice evil and die that is how people are going to 'cast and ban' you up and down and you will have no way to reside.

Now **I** have given more spirit souls to ban evil. Everybody who has the Holy Spirit will ban evils.

Anywhere you go they ban you.
You go left they ban you.
You go right they ban you.
You go up they ban you.
You come down they ban you.

You go front they ban you.
You go back they ban you.
You go to the middle they ban you.
You will have no way to go. So, stop practicing evil!

In your work place **I** ban all the evil people. *Amen!* In all the offices, all governments, all families and cities – Everywhere, Here and There, in spirit, in soul, in dream, **I** ban all the evil manipulations.

I ban all the witchcraft manipulations, all the reptiles' activities, all the satanic ways and activities. **I** have sent seventy-two million angels to ban all of them and you have become homeless. Since you have no way to live, you squat forever, in the name of our Lord Jesus Christ. Amen.

So, all principalities have squatted in the wastebasket with fire burning you. You will melt away because there is no home for you to survive. There is no food for you – no sacrifice for you anymore.

NO SACRIFICE ANYMORE! NO SACRIFICES ANYMORE!

THE SUPREME SACRIFICE is **THE BLOOD OF OUR LORD JESUS CHRIST**. Whenever anybody says, *'IN THE NAME AND BLOOD OF OUR LORD JESUS CHRIST'* that is the supreme sacrifice that **I** have made for everybody.

If you want to eat anything, eat fruit, vegetable, seed, herb and all other non living things. There is no more sacrifice of any kind. Sing songs of positive **WORD** and dance. That is the sacrifice for the Holy Spirit.

So, all the evil that go about deceiving people to go and throw things into the water, kill goat, do this and that are hungry souls. There is no food for them anymore, in the Name and Blood of our Lord Jesus Christ. Amen.

CONCLUSION B: **TO BELIEVE ANY OTHER THING APART FROM THE FATHER GOD IS AN INSULT**

The worst insult mankind can ever give to **ME, THE FATHER GOD** their Creator is to believe in inferior things – to believe that anything else exist apart from **THE FATHER GOD**. Look at such gross insult.

It can be likened unto a woman who believes that another man is her husband. What type of insult is that or a child that believes that someone somewhere is his father when in all aspects and in every indication, you are his father. You must call a spade a spade. What kind of insult is that? It is good to be serious – o!

Today, you must declare your seriousness, your conscience and your stand with **ME**. If you ever believe any other thing, call yourself any name – Jehovah or God, Emmanuel, spirit, man, good man, virgin, woman – whatsoever, it has no meaning to **ME, THE FATHER GOD**, your creator, if you believe any other thing apart from the **HOLY SPIRIT OF TRUTH**, the Spoken **WORD, THE FATHER GOD THE CREATOR OF THE UNIVERSE**,

This is how you will reason this –
Who created me?
Who created the whole world?
Who is living in the world?
Who controls the world?
Who is the Word?
What is THE SPIRIT?

So, if **THE FATHER GOD** exists and created the whole world filled the whole world with diverse amount of people then you must behave and respect **ME**. Look at how big the world is. Look at all the waters – Ocean, seas, rivers, streams, waterfalls etcetera, and look at the sky. Take in all **THE FATHER GOD'S** mighty creations as much as you possibly can, including you, then surrender to that Principal and that Phenomenon. You won't even see **HIM** but believe that **HE** lives in you because the **WORD** is in you.

Okay, view it in this dimension, is there anything that is done in this world that is not through **The WORD**? Everything is through **The WORD**. To list all the things that **The WORD** employs is more than tasking if not impossible, because it includes thoughts, actions, instructions, principles, formulas and nameless others. Everything seen and unseen are in the **WORD**.

The WORD is living in you. Even if you are barely surviving that little portion you use to survive everyday is from **The WORD**. Before anybody plans any evil for you, they would employ the **WORD** first in the thought so 'Cast and ban' that evil thought in him or her. That is the point of belief. When you do that you are free for eternity.

If after all this, you believe anything that **The WORD** created instead of believing **The WORD** then you are a wanted person and **I** count you as the least in this Kingdom.

CONCLUSION C: **WHAT MY SOUL HATES MOST**

I have revealed that the greatest insult to **THE FATHER GOD** is to believe something else than **THE FATHER GOD**. Look at a whole big person like you talking, commanding and doing everything as **GOD**, putting a small metal on your finger to protect you. Are you not ashamed of your self? Is that not you deceiving yourself?

You tie something around your waist as protection. You go to bow down to wood or stick or a stone somewhere. Stupid! That is idiot mind! Means get behind me stupid! There is nothing that is Satan than that type of believing as stupidity of the highest order. That is what Satan means- mistake. You believe an illusion as something that does not exist.

Therefore, from today all human beings on earth should take note that **I** have brought this to your attention.

It is a very shameful thing when someone writes negative words and publishes them and you buy the book and read it, copying the contents into you. In so doing you have invited some frustrated souls into you and your life takes a different turn.

Such writing occurs, because from time to time, the frustrated souls inspire people to write and from there they gain attention, and so have where to live. That is the reason there are secret societies everywhere.

You know that **THE FATHER GOD** eradicates evil so their period of operation is short and, because of that, they render you useless. What happens is that when they serve you, you also go to serve other people. Show **ME** any secret society that can come to **THE FATHER GOD**. All these prominent people are all in Satan's net one way or the other. Another Lecture Revelation that **I** will give is '*Those in Satan's Net*'

All the prominent people, especially those who have lots and lots of money have been captured by Satan because they think that Satan gave them the money that they have. The truth is that it is **GOD** that put them in that position, but Satan went and deceived them that saying, 'oh they are going to kill you. A lot of people are jealous of you. You know, before you were not rich, but now you are rich so many evil people will be after you.' Satan says that to people so that he will have glory from what **GOD** had already blessed.

Satan knew that Jesus Christ was The Creator as **The WORD**, become Man as the Father of all human beings' higherself on earth. In the second temptation, he pretended to be of help as he took Jesus to the top of the mountain. Then he asked Him to throw Himself down from there, that angels would bear Him up and even he himself Satan would catch Him from falling because 'all bow down to you and worship you, including me - Satan.'

Conqueror, Cover and The signature

You know, if Jesus Christ had listened to the negative voice and threw Him-self down, He would have died. You see that? The reason that would have occurred was that at that particular time Jesus had surrendered Himself to the negative self to test Him to see whether He would conquer the death on the cross.

You must prove yourself that you love **THE FATHER GOD ALMIGHTY** because this **CONQUERING** will not come until you have passed a test. That is what is happening. How will you pass the test? Use these **FATHER'S TALK (GOD PRESENT)** Lecture Revelations to elevate yourself. Stand with **THE FATHER GOD**; stand with The Truth. Persevere in tribulations; bear everything else and the temptations coming to you. These tests would only be for a short time. As long as you stand with **THE FATHER GOD** to the end, your future is bright.

Even now, **I** do not give access to any evil to tempt you, unless you put yourself there, because the blood of Christ has barricaded them.

Therefore, if there is anything **I** really hate, it is when you worship anything that is mundane as things that are not in existence. Instead of accepting to correct your mistake and reject the talisman that you are offered, you rather go ahead with the mistake and collect the item. What is the meaning of that? You put a small thing in your finger to protect you but how can that thing have energy to protect you? How did it manage? Who created you? So, the **ONE** that created you cannot protect you? Look at you!

In this world children attach themselves to their parents until they become adults. Thereafter, they take care of themselves. However, when a child runs away from home and hangs around with other runaways and vagabonds, there is something wrong with that child. Equally, if the father cannot take care of his child and the child runs away from home then, there is something wrong with that family.

Some children become headstrong because probably, their parents do not allow them to keep late nights or would not allow them to fornicate or misbehave in many other ways. So, these children would flaunt their parents' orders and leave home and hang out with undesirables. At this point they do not have a father again, because they have gone away from the umbrella of their father.

Any reasonable child that stays with his or her father will be under the umbrella of protection of their father. Do you know the reason you get involved in juju, secret societies, invocations and all sorts of things to protect yourself? It is because; –

You have refused to act according to the love of **GOD**.

You have refused to know **THE FATHER GOD**.

You have refused to love.
You have refused to be patient.
You have refused to be truthful.

Conqueror, Cover and The signature

You have refused to practice kindness.

You have refused to practice righteousness.

You fornicate, commit adultery, you kill and do all sorts of evil.

So, since you are negative you are afraid of life, because when you kill you shall be killed as such you join secret societies for protection; because you are afraid of the evils you do and have done. That is forced and false protection. Do you think that will by-pass **GOD**? You will still reap what you sow. The Law of Karma will still find you out no matter where you hide or how you struggle to camouflage yourself.

Therefore, do not worship any other thing and hope that **I** would shortlist you. You have already failed from the time you believe any other infidel things.

So, that is the Lecture Revelation that **I** given now to strengthen your faith. **I** also give this as a backing and a supporting energy, if you are a positive child of **THE FATHER GOD**, now and forever more. *Amen!*

LET **MY** PEACE AND BLESSING ABIDE WITH THE ENTIRE WORLD NOW AND FOREVER MORE, Amen.

THANK YOU FATHER.

Conqueror, Cover and The signature

Chapter Two

THE SPIRITUAL COVER
===============
MAXIMUM PROTECTION
MAXIMUM INSURANCE
MAXIMUM SECURITY

Conqueror, Cover and The signature

FATHER'S TALK
(GOD PRESENT)

Christ Our Lord, Twenty-third Simon Canaanite, FATHER, Two Thousand and Eight (BC/OB/BOOH) Saturday, Twenty-third February, Year Two Thousand and Eight (23/02/2008)

In the Name of Our Lord Jesus Christ In the Blood of Our Lord Jesus Christ Now and forever more

THE SPIRITUAL COVER
===================
MAXIMUM PROTECTION
MAXIMUM INSURANCE
MAXIMUM SECURITY

Today it pleases **ME, THE FATHER GOD THE CREATOR OF THE UNIVERSE** to give this Lecture Revelation. The title is **THE SPIRITUAL COVER (MAXIMUM**

PROTECTION, MAXIMUM INSURANCE AND MAXIMUM SECURITY).

INTRODUCTION

As **I** always advice anybody that reads **THE FATHER'S TALK** and however you come across **THE FATHER'S TALK**, clean your heart, clarify your conscience, be in spiritual self, conduct yourself with humility, because **THE FATHER'S TALK** is the **PRESENCE OF GOD. GOD** is The **WORD**.

When you start to read or listen to **THE FATHER'S TALK**, it does not matter how you come into contact with **THE FATHER'S TALK** and where you are, you are already in the Presence of your **FATHER GOD**, who is your inner self, which is your inner shrine. Your inner shrine is the **WORD**, which is **GOD** that lives in you. Since you have now taken evolution and joined this divine group as the divine section of rearranged human beings to read **THE FATHER'S**

TALK your life will turn for good. Because everybody that reads **THE FATHER'S TALK** must surely see a great change in his or her ways of life and even in their soul.

Since you are in possession of **THE FATHER'S TALK** and **I** cannot stress this enough - it does not matter how you come to be in possession of it. Whether by chance or accidental encounter or you made conscious and informed effort to acquire it, open your mind. In addition be positive and **THE FATHER GOD** will also open your intellect to understand as you listen to or read **THE FATHER'S TALK.** As a result you are able to imbibe the words of **THE FATHER'S TALK** and it will elevate your spirit.

All **THE FATHER'S TALK** has something to do with your spirit, your soul and your physical life including your understanding. It is for your higher self, your higher consciousness - higher soul so as to know what you are doing and how to treat life generally.

I brought this idea on earth so that **I** will lead every person back to **MYSELF**, because **I** use The **WORD** to create everything and The **WORD** lives in humans. This idea can be likened unto the television or radio box in your house. You are the receiver of the **WORD**. **I AM** giving the **WORD** and you are receiving the **WORD** into yourself that will change your environment for good.
Thereafter, you and **I** become one – positive, positive, positive!

A: **MAXIMUM PROTECTION OF THE FATHER GOD**

This Lecture Revelation is advance of **THE CONQUEROR**. This is **The COVER** for children of **GOD**. People of **GOD** are always afraid and because of that, they are forced to do what they are not supposed to do.

People find it difficult to believe that someone can live life naturally, without believing in idols or believing in any other thing and without taking prescribed drugs, tablets or any mundane medication. **I** can prove to you that His Royal Majesty King Solomon David Jesse **ETE** and his family live naturally and there many other people like that that live a natural life. They don't take any medicine. They do not go to hospital because **THE FATHER GOD** is their doctor.

THE FATHER GOD is the hospital and everything for them. The only thing is that they have to be careful with what they eat and how they live their lives. If you live carelessly you will go to careless place with similar people to take care of you. As a rearranged human being, you need to live with rearranged people. The Holy Spirit is a rearranged phenomenon.

If you are living according to the tenets of the Holy Spirit and you want to eat something and the Holy Spirit asks you not to eat it because it will cause you to be ill then you must stop. You want to say a word and the Holy Spirit says, don't say this word because it is negative then you must stop. That is **THE SPIRITUAL COVER**.

THE SPIRITUAL COVER is the Holy Spirit. **THE SPIRITUAL COVER** is everything good. The Holy Spirit is everything for you. When **I** talk about the **Maximum Protection** of **THE FATHER GOD** for all human beings as those who believe in **THE FATHER GOD**, it is the Holy Spirit.

The Holy Spirit lives in you and stays with you because you do not have any other belief apart from **HIM**. And it is because you have maximized your heart with **HIM** and not minimized. When you maximize your heart with **THE FATHER GOD**, it means that you put yourself high with **GOD** and with the trust. Maximising yourself with **THE FATHER GOD** means you test **GOD** to see whether **HE** exists.

You know when you maximize yourself with something, it as when you see advertisement about a new product such as a type of food that fancy. You will see the beautiful presentation and how inviting the food appears, and then you maximize your heart to taste that food. The taste of the pudding is by eating. If you do not taste the food you would not know how delicious the food is or not as the case maybe.

Maximum Protection of **GOD** is when you fully in all your hope and in all your faith believe **THE FATHER GOD** and that too is how you trust **GOD** so a trial of this means to maximize you're thought on that. How do you do this? Try having implicit faith and hope in **THE FATHER GOD** and see. People have been staying without tasting the pudding so what do you think?

You want to override it and force the situation, just like those who force-ripe fruits. They pluck unripe fruits and use chemicals to ripen them unnaturally. Sometimes they freeze the fruits and flowers. They would spray red liquid substance on red flowers to become extra red. That is not natural.

Some people engineer food and call it GM food but that is not natural. Such food has side effects and it destroys the inside of human beings. So, if you want to protect yourself, be careful with what you eat. Be careful with what you say because if you say evil words the evil words will boomerang on you. If you plan evil on someone the evil will come back to you. Then you would say, 'oh why has **THE FATHER GOD** not protected me.' How can **THE FATHER GOD** protect **HIMSELF** in you when you have already destroyed yourself in **THE FATHER GOD**? Don't you know that everything you do boomerangs on you.

For all the countries that go to war, war awaits them. If you do anything, do it in a good way because just prepare yourself for the same because it will surely boomerang on you. If you do good things, no matter how long it takes you will reap the good things. If you do bad things no matter how long it takes, it will come back to you and you will reap that bad thing, unless you replace the bad thing with good things.

So, all those who hear or read **THE FATHER'S TALK (GOD PRESENT)** and have heard this today and want to take **THE COVER OF GOD MAXIMUM PROTECTION OF THE FATHER GOD** but know that yesterday you perpetrated wickedness on people hate people thought evil for people and did all sorts of negative things then start to do good things today. Start to love. Start to be peaceful. Start to think well and speak well and do well and hear well. You would only be hearing good, good things now. Start to practice oneness and be merciful on people. When you do all these things, you claim lots of points because you claim points for doing good things. And that will automatically replace the debts of all the negative things that you practiced before. That is the only way of escape.

B: **MAXIMUM INSURANCE**

The insurance for your soul is when you practice love then; you are one with **THE FATHER GOD.** When you practice peace, you are a peacemaker. ***Blessed are the peacemakers for they shall be called children of GOD***. Being a child of **GOD** means The **WORD** will always be by your side and protect you.

Blessed are the merciful for they shall obtain mercy. That means you gather insurance for yourself when you practice mercy. Because wherever you go The **WORD** in you that you promote, as **Mercy** will always stand by you and will obtain mercy at the crucial needing point of your life. You will not face any disappointment. The **WORD** will prove **HIMSELF** to you to be Mercy and be merciful to you. You know this **WORD** is true. Try and see and **HE** will never fail you.

So, the **Maximum Insurance** is when you have oneness, you share what you have with people and **I** with good people. The **WORD** in turn will share all **HE** has with you. Let's say that The **WORD** knows that you have one hundred pounds but out of that, you take forty pounds or so to help poor people. That means **THE FATHER GOD** will insure the sixty pounds for you. And **HE** will always give you more and more money. You will never lack income because the insurance of your income is as a result of you sharing with people. The **WORD** knows this in your heart. You do not need to tell anybody because inside you there is a spirit of monitor, which is the Spoken Word that monitors all your actions. Regardless that **the WORD** lives in you, **HE** gives you the freewill to act so that you can enjoy **HIM** because if not **I** would be directing people. Don't you know that?

Conqueror, Cover and The signature

Sometimes, when you have the high spirit, the spirit takes over and directs you, whether positive or negative. The reason **I** allow you normal life is so that you have freedom. **I** will thereafter come and sign for you and that is **Maximum Insurance**. Practice oneness, love, mercy, peace and kindness and forgive one another. Live a good life with people. Let people get **THE FATHER'S TALK (GOD PRESENT)** through you. Give out good news to people. Do not hide them because these are the insurances that you attract to yourself under this **SPIRITUAL COVER**.

C: MAXIMUM SECURITY

Security is the power of **GOD** through faith. When you have faith in **THE FATHER GOD** and you believe that, everything you do is good then good follows you. **Do good= good follow you; do bad = bad follow you: simple.**

The **WORD** is not a respecter of anyone, because you cannot bribe the **WORD**. You can do everything in this world, but you cannot bribe The **WORD – THE SPIRIT** because **HE** is in your conscience. With that understanding, humankind must surely sort to protect everything they do in order to have it. You must believe that the Holy Spirit of **GOD** in you is the **Maximum Security**.

It is the Holy Spirit of **GOD** in you that are securing you as Truth. Truth is the point at which the Holy Spirit of **GOD** secures you for **HIMSELF**. If you have the Spirit of truth and believe the truth then, the Holy Spirit will always protect you. Stand on the side of truth. Read the Lecture Revelation titled '***THE SPIRIT OF TRUTH'*** and the Lecture Revelation titled '***POST, POSITION AND NAME.***'

The Holy Spirit is Truth. The Truth means security. The only thing that will make the Holy Spirit to always stand by you when you have faith in

HIM is when you are truthful. Do not deviate from the truth side of **THE FATHER GOD** because that is the true side of you.

So, all the people that look for **COVER** elsewhere and try to take protection anywhere else through doing 'assignments', and all sorts of things have failed because you look for **COVER** where you cannot get it. That person you go to, who **COVERS** them? Where is the insurance of the person you go to for **COVER**? These people do not really **COVER** you. They would ask you to pay lots of money and do sacrifices. You are the one that does all those things and not them.

The only way you can **COVER** yourself is with **THE FATHER GOD, THE SUPREME ENTITY** and it is for you to love one another. That is the connection. That is the deal. Now, **I** have brought the most straightforward and simplest way to take **COVER** with **THE FATHER GOD, THE CREATOR OF THE UNIVERSE.**

This is by joining **THE SUPREME WORD CELEBRATION SEASON** and recognizing **THE FATHER GOD** as **THE WORD, THE CREATOR OF THE UNIVERSE**. When you do this, you have **COVER** and you have secured yourself. This is why **I** want the true children of **GOD** to come together in love. Forgive yourselves. Read the Lecture Revelation titled, **IN-BETWEEN THE FATHER AND THE SON THERE IS A SERVANT**. Muslims and Christians must come together as they are from one father and one mother and are therefore the children of the same parent. It is necessary for you to have peace, because without this you destroy yourself.

No security for anyone who hates another person.

No security for those who go to war.

No security for those who suppress people.

No security for those who hate people.

No security for those who engage in tribalism.

No security for those who engage in segregation.

No security for those who cause division.

No security for those who are jealous.

No security for those who strife.

No security for those who kill.

No security for those who practice wickedness of any kind.

Security is for those who make peace.

Security is for those who believe in truth.

Security is for those who are merciful.

Security is for those who are patient and patiently wait for the Will of GOD to manifest in them.

Security is for those who practice righteousness, charity and are merciful, helping the poor and the needy.

These are the **Maximum Securities** that **I** given to people. So if you practice what is good, good things will come to you. If you practice what is bad, bad will follow you. It does not matter the name you call it or how you dress up, bad is bad. If you like fast everyday but if you do not forgive one another then the hatred spirit in you will consume your fasting.

You know, sin consumes a lot of energy. It is like the capacity of a battery and the volume of energy of consumption. When the volume of something is too big, that is, bigger than the voltage, the capacity of the voltage cannot carry it. So, any small energy or additional energy that will be introduced to you will be completely used up. Sin uses up a lot of energy in a person. That is the reason for sacrifices that they ask you for as goat, sheep and chicken and so on. These things are insatiable and the next thing you know you kill your child and kill yourself and so on and so forth and those who do not sacrifice in these ways give their sacrifices through more sexual acts and it goes on and on.

The only energy that is free and you will not even know it's there like the general electricity supply, is love. Also inclusive are peace, mercy, oneness and forgiveness. Forgive one another. If you do all these good things and live a simple life and believe in only **THE FATHER GOD** then, **THE FATHER GOD will** give you that insurance and complete assurance of **HIS** security. And that means it is the same security that **THE FATHER GOD** has is the same security that you will *COVER* yourself.

D: ACTIVATION OF THE ABOVE

How do you activate the above energy of **GOD** in you that is, **Maximum Protection, Maximum Insurance and Maximum Security**? How do you activate them?

To activate the above components in you is to start from now to believe that only **THE FATHER GOD** exists.

Have love for one another. Have patience. Join HRM King Solomon for the celebration of **The Universal Supreme Word Season**. When you do that that is the beginning of knowing who your **FATHER GOD** is.

Worship **THE FATHER GOD** in spirit and in truth and believe that there is nothing like incantation among other diabolical activities because they do not work.

Resign from all secret cults and secret societies. Fully disgrace all negative spiritual activities that you are involved in including the witchcraft that you have joined and practice. Maybe someone gave it to you or you joined because of the threat of death or that they frightened you. Disgrace them. Confess openly and cut-off from them because when you do that, you have activated the protection of **GOD** in you. **GOD** is always there.

Let **ME** tell you something, if you have a functioning torchlight with a battery in it in your hand but you do not switch it on, it will not light up. If the torchlight is the winding type and you do not wind it, it will not work, but the energy is there. The option is there for the activation. Also, if you take a picture with a camera and you do not develop the films to view the pictures they will remain there in the film negative. For anything you have, there is something you have to do to activate it so as to make good use of it. So, to activate the above, you must **LOVE ONE ANOTHER**. You must believe **THE FATHER GOD**. You must listen to **THE FATHER'S TALK**. You must direct yourself to the path of God – the Holy Spirit of Truth. There is no compromise at all. No compromise of evil.

    Come closer to **THE FATHER'S TALK** (**GOD PRESENT**) as the Voice of **GOD** in the latter day. Then you will see that this is **The Everlasting Testimony for Everlasting Gospel of God – The Word of God.** Celebrate **The Universal Supreme Word Season Celebration.** That is signing in to the **WORD.** When you do this you have automatically activated the power of God in you in the three capacities namely, **Maximum Protection, Maximum Insurance and Maximum Security.** Then you will be sleeping soundly. So soundly, you are like *nso ke nkekere - nso ke nkekere* (literally – what do I think about –what do I think about, that is to say no worries at all) all the time. You will not worry because peace of **GOD** will be around you all the time and protect you since peace is the word of **GOD** that you are promoting.

Promote this **FATHER'S TALK (GOD PRESENT)** in every way, through cash and kind. Promote it in the maximum way. Make it possible for other people to enjoy it as you. Support the whole innovation. Let the whole world join this campaign of **THE FATHER GOD, THE CELEBRATION OF THE UNIVERSAL SUPREME WORD SEASON** that will change the whole world for good forever. That is the activation of the above.

When you help widows, when you help those who are hungry, when you help the poor, the elderly and those in need (personally help them and think well about them in a positive way) then you have activated the above.

The **Security** and **Insurance** and **Protection** lie on you trusting **THE HOLY SPIRIT OF TRUTH** - trusting **THE FATHER GOD** and handing over yourself for **THE FATHER GOD** to take care of you, because **HE** is your creator. If you believe that the **ONE** that created you has your spare parts and **HE** can protect your soul then, know that you have the above and you have activated them.

When you have activated them, you will see the flavour of **THE HOLY SPIRIT OF TRUTH** in you. There will be signs. Do not be disturbed about some dreams. Evil will show you bad things, but believe **ME** that if you ignore all that and worship **THE FATHER GOD** in spirit and in truth you have conquered already and are, in the Name and Blood of Our Lord Jesus Christ.

There is **Maximum Power, Security** and **Insurance** in this **FATHER'S TALK (GOD PRESENT)**.

This **FATHER'S TALK** itself is **Security.**

This **FATHER'S TALK** itself is **Insurance.**

This **FATHER'S TALK** itself is **Protection.**

If you have a copy of this **FATHER'S TALK (GOD PRESENT)** and you believe every word in it, then automatically you are ***COVERED***. It will protect you because it is the Word of **GOD**.

This is **FATHER'S TALK (GOD PRESENT)** and it means **I, MYSELF** yielding **the Everlasting Energy** of **Protection, Insurance and Security** for all positive humans on earth. Therefore, you must have a copy.

Your child must have a copy.
Your wife must have a copy.
Your husband must have a copy.

Everybody must have a copy as **Insurance**, as **Protection,** and as **Security**.

You are not to worship the paper, but you must believe the words inside them. This is not a secret word of a secret society. This Word is to believe the Spoken Word. This Word is to practice not having a book and worshiping it, but you are having the contents, which consist of the wisdom, the understanding, the spirit of love and the spirit of peace and of humility and of forgiveness.

If you have one million of these books in you and you do not believe these **Words** and so do not put any into practice, then the next day even a rat will drive you away from your house. However, if you have these **Words** in you and believe in them and then practice them, then you gain the above components of **THE FATHER GOD**. Then you must know that **THE FATHER GOD** is in you and wants you to be good and encourages you to love, to be a peacemaker, not

Conqueror, Cover and The signature

to go to war, not to suppress people and stand by the truth and always be truthful. Forgive one another, have mercy, help people, practice oneness and make everything good with everybody. Then **Maximum Security** mentioned above, including, **Maximum Insurance** and **Maximum Protection** is your free gift, in the Name of Our Lord Jesus Christ. Amen.

When you actually want to activate this in the practical terms, knock your head three times on the ground, wherever you find yourself. Do not face any particular way or direction. Everywhere is everywhere. Everywhere, here and there is **THE FATHER GOD. HE** is in you. **HE** is the Divine atmosphere of Life, and **HE** is the everlasting atmosphere of Peace, **THE SUPREME WORD**.

When you knock your head on the ground for **THE FATHER GOD,** confess all your sins as anything you know that is wrong.

You hate people.

Conqueror, Cover and The signature

You gossip.
You tarnish people's name.
You kill
You fornicate
You steal and do all sorts of bad things.
You commit abortion and do many other bad things.
You suppress people
You do all sorts of unacceptable things in the office.
You tell lies
You take bribes
You siphon money.
You are cunning.
You do lots of things that you know are sinful.

When you know you do all these things and your conscience blames you then apologise in your heart. To whom should you apologise?

You apologise to **ME, THE FATHER GOD THE CREATOR OF THE UNIVERSE**, the ONE that is talking to you now. When you do this confess and talk to **ME, THE FATHER GOD**, talk to **ME** as though you are talking to yourself. Talk to **GOD** as though you are talking to yourself and when you are done, then leave everything to **THE FATHER GOD**.

When you kneel down you hold **MY** feet because the earth is the feet of **THE FATHER GOD** while the Heaven is the Throne of **THE FATHER GOD**, but you cannot reach Heaven, but you can reach **MY** feet. When you hold **MY** feet **I** will know that somebody needs **MY** attention. Then **I** will come to you and forgive you.

You would then come to understand and believe that our Lord Jesus Christ was the Father Adam's higher spirit that came to die. **HE** was the **SUPREME WORD** that became flesh. **HE** was that same **SUPREME WORD** that lived in Adam. Since Adam sinned, **THE SUPREME WORD** THE HOLY SPIRIT OF TRUTH was no longer living in Adam, which made Adam incomplete SUPER HUMAN GOD.

So, that Higher Spirit of Adam came back as the **TOTAL WORD THE**

CREATOR OF THE UNIVERSE and died to salvage Adam and all other human beings. Do you believe this story? This story is a fact. If you believe this story, then instantly the Blood of Christ washes you clean and you stand a chance of a new evolution to a new life in the SUPREME FUTURE. And you are surely protected. That means that you are baptised in spirit and that means that **Maximum Security, Maximum Protection and Maximum Insurance** are activated right there in you and protects you, now and forever more. Amen.

E: WHAT MAKES YOU DIFFERENT FROM OTHER HUMAN BEINGS

The above activation is the **Word of GOD** as faith and the Holy Spirit in you. That will make you a different human being on earth.

Being truthful makes you a different human on earth.

Being merciful makes you a different human on earth.

Being honest makes you a different human on earth. Being happy, loving and practicing oneness, righteousness will make you a different human being on earth. Always be peaceful. Be a peacemaker. All these stars make you a different human being on earth.

Read the Lecture Revelation titled **INDESTRUCTIBLE PHENOMENON FIVE STARS** then you will know this. Also, read the Lecture Revelation titled **THE FOETUS OF THE NEW KINGDOM**, and then you will know that when you bear these fruits you are a different human being on earth. Different human beings are those who **THE FATHER GOD** is activated in them as **GOD PRESENT**. They are those who put on Christ; those who believe in truth; those who believe in faith and have faith and those who are honest, positive human beings.

You must be different from:
Those who practice wickedness and
Those who are idol worshippers,

Those who use talisman,

Those who hang things on their neck for protection

Those who wear other things for protection,

Those who bury things in the ground and

those who are disgrace themselves and many other diabolical things people do. **I** will change them from human beings to human animals, since they believe that those things can protect them.

In contrast, those who believe that **THE FATHER GOD** is their **GOD AND SPIRITUAL FATHER, THE SUPREME ENERGY, THE SUPREME WORD** that lives in them, with connection to 'love one another', with connection to appreciation of the **SUPREME WORD** and join the celebration of **THE SUPREME WORD**, are different human beings. There is activated spirit of **GOD** in you in earnest as a result.

F: **YOU CANNOT HAVE COVER FOR BEING DOUBLE-FACED**

I cannot **COVER** you if you are double-faced. Today you worship **GOD**. Tomorrow you would go to worship idol. Today you do assignment in the house of an evil man tomorrow you come to **THE FATHER GOD.**

Sign on with **ME**, with faith and with Truth because **I AM** based on the Spoken Word alone. If you go to worship anything that the **WORD** created instead of worshiping the **SUPREME WORD HIMSELF,** then you are worshipping elementary spirit souls. In this regard you are double-faced. You are two-faced. Since you are two-faced, your faith swings around. You cannot therefore be covered with this potency. The **OOO** means **Maximum Protection, Maximum Insurance** and **Maximum Security.**

This is **GOD** of Heaven, **GOD** of the Soul and **GOD** of the Earth. This also means the Spoken Word – **The Father, Son and the Holy Spirit.** This also means everything that exists. This also means Omnipotent, Omnipresent, and Omniscience. This is **THE FATHER GOD HIMSELF** in **Maximum Potency**.

If you want this power to **COVER** you from generation upon generation and you become a member of the **Great Positive Family** called **Ete Royal Universal Family of Brotherhood of the Cross and Star**, then you must surely lose one face. All those who join secret societies should refrain from them and any such related societies.

Refrain from wickedness.

Refrain from tribalism and all manner of segregation

Refrain from strife.

Refrain from jealousy.

Refrain from gossiping,

Refrain from damaging people's name.

Refrain from reporting people wrongly.

Refrain from going to see native doctors.

Refrain from going to see soothsayers and palm readers.

Refrain from doing evil assignments and all sorts of other evil things.

When you refrain from all these practices then **I** will **COVER** you. But if you go here, and there, you will not get this **COVER** and blame yourself if anything happens to your soul.

When you refuse to pay your electric bills for instance, they cut your supply. Although you could probably get yourself a generator, but when the fuel in the generator finishes or the fan belt cuts, it renders the generator inoperable and you would not have light. Then you would notice the difference.

However, the small amount you pay for the supply of general electricity will give you constant light and with no equipment maintenance hassles and no noise, unlike the generator operated one. As you are not the one that maintains the general electric supply you are free from such responsibility.

Today, if you believe **THE FATHER GOD,** join **The Universal Supreme Word Celebration** with HRM King Solomon **ETE**. You do not therefore need to do any other sacrifice. The Blood of Christ, which is the Spoken Word, has **COVERED** you.

I will use your kind donation, whether in kind or cash as well as your appreciation in words, power and attention in believing the **WORD,** including your appreciation in love, in charity, in mercy, in oneness and in all the things you do positively. **I** will use them as your gesture to utilize the opportunity to sign on with **THE FATHER GOD** to *COVER* you. 'Nothing goes for nothing.' Everything in this world goes with something. Since you have faith and recognize **THE FATHER GOD**, that is your donation and **GOD** will use that to *COVER* you.

No double-faced individuals can gain from this. If you have no faith or have lost faith with **THE FATHER GOD** forget about getting **THE SPIRITUAL COVER** of **THE FATHER GOD**.

G: **CALL A SPADE A SPADE**

You think that because you bring money to **GOD** you can go to worship idols? **I** know that many people in this world build houses for **GOD** and do lots of things for **GOD** but they also go to see people who practice witchcraft and, native doctors to perform incantations and so on to protect them. Who actually protects you? Do you think **I** share with rubbish?

From the day **I** know you meet another man **I** will not touch you again. From the day **I** know you meet another woman **I** will not touch you again. **I AM** not that type of man and **I AM** not that type of woman. Anybody in this world that goes to look for any power other than that of **THE FATHER GOD** to *COVER* him or her, then that is the end of you and **ME**. Nonetheless, you will still survive according to the natural energy of life, because every human being that is born into this world has stipulated days of life. That is the reason some evil people say – 'but I do all this evil and I am still alive. I kill and I have not died. I practice wickedness and I am not dead. I am a witch or a wizard and I have not died.'

Do you know what is taking place? You have one time loan of life. Could be you are to spend maybe sixty or eighty or one hundred years in this world. As it is, you are using those years to practice evil since you are not dead. What is **MY** concern? Your loan is still there - your loan of time for living. When your time is finished then you would know you wasted your time.

You are here on earth and have not practiced any positive thing and you say you are still living? What do you think will happen to you? For some of you, when it is close to the end of your life that is when you see the sign of your wickedness showing in you. Some of you exit this world early and quickly without seeing the folly of your wickedness. Still, when you are born again into this world your basket will be waiting for you because nobody goes free. You pay for all your actions. You reap exactly what you sow.

Call a spade a spade. You cannot bribe the Holy Spirit. You cannot bribe **THE FATHER GOD**. Anything you sow that is what you reap.

If you give a deaf ear to all this information and all this wisdom, then it is up to you. It means that is what is written about you. That is what suits you. But those who **THE FATHER GOD** gives ability to change their minds and take action, **THE FATHER GOD** will also take action and give them the opportunity to take evolution for positivism that will help their soul and their life for eternity.

CONCLUSION A: **THOU SHALL NOT HAVE ANY OTHER GOD BUT THE FATHER GOD.**

THOU SHALL NOT HAVE ANY OTHER GOD APART FROM **THE FATHER GOD.**
THAT IS THE ORDER!
As little or tiny or as big as that object could be, thou shall not have it as your **GOD**. All **THE FATHER GOD'S** children must believe in themselves. Believe in **THE FATHER GOD** in you and you have **MY SPIRITUAL *COVER***. Do not go to hang anything around your body or do all sorts of odd things because you will fail for doing that.

CONCLUSION B: **THOU SHALL NOT BOW TO ANYTHING MAN MADE AS SOMETHING TO PROTECT YOU.**

You should never bow down to anything manmade and call it

protection because it is an insult to **THE FATHER GOD**. Do not have any talisman with you or put on rings as a source of protection. Do not do anything to protect you. Believe that **The Sure Foundation Stone of Protection is The WORD OF GOD** and the Holy Spirit of **THE FATHER GOD** is in you to protect you. When you do that you are surely saved.

CONCLUSION C: **PROVE YOURSELF, AND I, THE FATHER GOD WILL AM SERIOUS WITH YOU.**

If you prove yourself as a positive child of **THE FATHER GOD** –
As one that wants to know more and
wants to come closer to **THE FATHER GOD.**
wants to worship **THE FATHER GOD**
wants to know **THE FATHER GOD** –
wants improvement in your spiritual life and

want to be a positive child of **THE FATHER GOD** now and in future, then join this teaching.

Believe these teachings.

Believe this is **THE FATHER'S TALK (GOD PRESENT)**.

Believe in **The Supreme Word Season Celebration.** Believe in The Trinity **GOD**, THE WORD in you, and THE BLOOD in you and THE WATER in you.

Believe in love and peace and faith and oneness and goodness. Do what is good.

You know what is good. Even though you say there is nothing like **GOD**, you believe in **GOOD**. You believe in the **WORD.** Just believe in the word of your mouth as positive words. Speak positively, speak well, think well and do well and hear well. Take yourself away from negativism as anything evil, then you are surely saved.

LET **MY** PEACE AND BLESSING ABIDE WITH THE ENTIRE WORLD NOW AND FOREVER MORE. AMEN.

THANK YOU FATHER. THANK YOU FATHER. THANK YOU FATHER

In the Name of Our Lord Jesus Christ
In the Blood of Our Lord Jesus Christ
Now and forever more

Song:
He's the Supreme Word OOO
*　　He's the Supreme Word*
*　　The Word of the universe*
*　　Leader Olumba Olumba Obu*

He's the Supreme Word OOO
*　　He's the Supreme Word*
*　　The Word of the universe*
*　　Leader Olumba Olumba Obu*

THANK YOU FATHER

Conqueror, Cover and The signature

Chapter Three

THE SIGNATURE (MY STAMP, MY APPROVAL MY SEAL AND DELIVERY)

Conqueror, Cover and The signature

FATHER'S TALK
(GOD PRESENT)
Date: OB/OB/OH: The second day of the second month of THE FATHER (year) two thousand and eight

In the Name of Our Lord Jesus Christ
In the Blood of Our Lord Jesus Christ
Now and forever more,

THE SIGNATURE (MY STAMP, MY APPROVAL MY SEAL AND DELIVERY)

THE SIGNATURE OF THE FATHER GOD THE CREATOR OF THE UNIVERSE.

Today it pleases **ME THE FATHER GOD THE CREATOR OF THE UNIVERSE, THE SUPREME WORD OF THE UNIVERSE** as **THE FATHER, THE SON** and **THE HOLY SPIRIT** to earmark this day that HRM King Solomon has put aside to thank **THE**

FATHER GOD as his own **CREATOR**. The title of today's revelation is, **THE SIGNATURE OF THE FATHER GOD THE CREATOR OF THE UNIVERSE, MY STAMP, MY SEAL, AND MY APPROVAL AND DELIVERY**. When **I** tick **RIGHT** or **X** then that is the end of that matter.

A: INTRODUCTION

Today's Revelation Lecture is about the **FIVE PRINCIPLES** that **I** have in **MY ENTITY** as **MY OWN SELF**. These are the **PRINCIPLES OF ME**, **THE FATHER GOD THE CREATOR OF THE UNIVERSE** and they are **MY SIGNATURE, MY STAMP** and **MY SEAL** when **I APPROVE** something. From here, **I** will give the order for **DELIVERY**. The concept is that once **I APPROVE** something that is the end of it. If you see anything shakeable, or anything going on that can be seen, heard or touched then you should know that it is the will of **THE FATHER GOD**. It may not please everybody, because the situation may not be good for people or it may be negative or **POSITIVE** but **I THE FATHER GOD** knows the secret of why **HE** allows the event to take place or for that thing to happen. **I AM** using this opportunity to make all the humans **GOD'S** and all **POSITIVE** children of **GOD** know that they should be **CALM** in every situation, be **HAPPY** and rejoice when anything happens because that is the will of **I THE FATHER GOD**.

Nothing on earth is ever the will of man, or Satan's will. No phenomenon or man has a will. **THE FATHER GOD** alone knows the reason why any event takes place and **I** will use it to **GLORIFY MYSELF** at the end of it, but man must have long **PATIENCE** to be able to wait and see what will be the end of that situation.

Sometimes when something happens, evil people think that it is part of their plan because they think that they have gotten away with it or they have succeeded, but at the end of it, we shall know whether it is **THE FATHER GOD** or they that made that thing to be as it is. This Revelation Lecture is to educate all children of **GOD**. If you really, really believe in **GOD** you must reach this point.

The **WILL OF GOD** is events that takes place in any form and whenever you pray and do everything, and even talk to **GOD** about the situation and **GOD** does not change the situation; take it with **GOOD FAITH**, because **I THE FATHER GOD** knows why **I** allow that thing to take place. And that is what **I** want everybody to know so that you can **UNDERSTAND**, **LOVE**, **BELIEVE** and **KNOW GOD** by reaching this stage in **LIFE** and in **CONSCIOUSNESS**. The meaning of **FAITH** and **BELIEVING** in **THE FATHER GOD** is when you attribute every event, every situation and every happening to be the **APPROVAL** of **GOD**.

B: **MY STAMP**

I want to reveal that before **I APPROVE** anything, **I** need to see a **STAMP**. There are two types of **STAMPS** that exist. There is the negative or **POSITIVE STAMP**, but the first **STAMP** is **POSITIVE**. Every office has a **STAMP**, and in **MY** system as **THE FATHER GOD THE CREATOR OF THE UNIVERSE**, there are two existing **STAMPS**. One is **POSITIVE** and the other is negative. The two of them are in **MY** office called **CHRIST**, and that office is the **SPOKEN WORD**. Today **I** want to reveal one important thing that you may not understand that it but is very, very, very important.

In **MY** office of **CHRIST**, **I** have two **STAMPS** as carves and in the back of one **STAMP**, the inscription is the **SUPREME WORD** and the front of this **STAMP**, there is another inscription which says **THE POSITIVE**

SUPREME WORD and on the other **STAMP** the inscription says, **THE SUPREME WORD**: negative word. This means that the **WORD** has two **STAMPS** and one is **POSITIVE** and the other is negative. And where the **STAMP** is inscribed is in the mind of man. It is like a rubber **STAMP** and the **STAMP** is the mind where the **WORD** is. The human mind has an inscription as **POSITIVE** and negative and that is **MY STAMP** as **THE STAMP OF SUPREME WORD**, and **THE FATHER GOD THE CREATOR OF THE UNIVERSE**. When the mind conceives an idea or a plan in the physical reality through **THINKING** or **REASONING** as a conceived **THOUGHT**, it may be **POSITIVE** or negative, and that is the **STAMP** that is carved, but you must put it down in the face of **THE FATHER GOD** for **APPROVAL**.

The first thing is the idea as a conceived **THOUGHT** in the mind. The next thing is what you want to do with this **THOUGHT**? Usually, you want an event to take place and you know from your mind whether the event will be **POSITIVE** or negative. When you have an idea in your mind and want that event to take place, it means that you have put the **STAMP** on the sheet of paper. When you make a pronouncement of that idea, as the **WORD** then you have brought it to the general public, because you want **THE FATHER GOD** to **APPROVE** it for everybody to obey that **WORD**. In the paper which is your mind or atmosphere in-between human beings on earth, the **APPROVAL** of **THE FATHER GOD**, is the event that will take place in the **POSITIVE** way. After that, you would want the event to work, because the **STAMP** is the **WORD** that has been carved as a negative or **POSITIVE** idea generating with the force of the **WORD**. It means that inside of you, the idea has generated in your mind with the force of the **SPOKEN WORD**.

You will then put the idea across to **THE FATHER GOD** and request that **I** should **APPROVE** it. And eventually the **APPROVAL** of the **WORD** will come through a fellow human being like you, but that is **THE FATHER GOD**. This means that the event is **APPROVED**, in a physical way. **I** want everybody to be humble and be in spirit, so that you can understand this Lecture Revelation, because it is a bit deeper. People always ask why **THE FATHER GOD** allows this and that to happen and why **HE APPROVES** this and that. Today, you will know that when you think and plan evil, it comes to pass and sometimes you think that it is **THE FATHER GOD** that wants it to pass and of cause yes, it is **THE FATHER GOD**, but you first passed that event.

C: **THE APPROVAL**

The (**APPROVAL**) is by the **SPOKEN WORD** as the **WORD** that you have pronounced. When you conceive the **THOUGHT**, you bring it to fruition by **PRONOUNCING** the **WORD** out. As soon as you **PRONOUNCE** the **WORD**, you have made the **WORD** to **APPROVE** that event, because the **WORD** must surely come to pass. When the idea dies off in your mind, in other **WORDS** when you change your mind after the **THOUGHT**, then the **SUPREME WORD** has not been **APPROVED**. However as soon as you make a **PRONOUNCEMENT** of what is in your mind either **POSITIVE** or negative, then it has been **STAMPED** and it must surely come to pass as a **POSITIVE** or a negative occurrence. As soon as you make a **PRONOUNCEMENT**, it is **APPROVED**, but that does not mean that **I** have **SIGNED** it, because that is the mystery in-between the **SPOKEN WORD**.

When you make a **PRONOUNCEMENT**, it means that it

Conqueror, Cover and The signature

has taken an **APPROVAL**, but that **APPROVAL** requires a **SIGNATURE**.

For instance, if you apply for a grant through an officer that works in the branch of the company, where applications are made, the officer will first sort out your application locally and **APPROVE** it. However after the **APPROVAL** of the officer, the application needs to be **SIGNED** by an **AUTHORISED** person. There must be a **SIGNATURE**, and **SEAL** before you can finally have what you have requested for, however, it is **APPROVED**. This is known as **APPROVED** in principle. Those who work in the bank use this system. This means that there are things that they still want to check as **POSITIVE** or negative. The principle of the **WORD** is that as soon as you make a **PRONOUNCEMENT**, the **WORD** **APPROVES** it whether it is **GOOD** or bad, and that is the **POWER** of the **SPOKEN WORD, THE SUPREME WORD**.

The **WORD APPROVES** all **PRONOUNCEMENTS** provided they are made. It does not matter if it is **GOOD** or bad, because that is the **POWER** of the **SPOKEN WORD, THE SUPREME WORD.** And when the **WORD APPROVES, HE** sends the ideas or thought to **THE FATHER GOD** for a final **SIGNATURE. THE FATHER GOD** is the **TRUTH** and that is when the **APPROVAL** ends if it is not truthful. But the **APPROVAL** starts when the **PRONOUNCEMENT** is made.

From today, you should know this so that you will not say that you are sorry because you made a mistake. You should know that any **PRONOUNCEMENT** that you make means that you have **APPROVED** that thing. The only thing that you can do is to call back and replace your **WORD** with another **WORD,** if you know that you made a mistake and say anything that you are not supposed to say and then revoke it. In this case, the two kinds of **WORD** will come to pass; it means that you have **APPROVED** two things, the first **WORD** and the second **WORD**. The two of them will then come to struggle for **THE FATHER'S SIGNATURE**, and that is the confusion that comes into the whole world. And this is why politicians cannot worship **GOD**, and lawyers cannot be **TRUTHFUL** with the **HOLY SPIRIT OF TRUTH**, because they are joking with the **WORD**.

I have said this many times that if you want to be really **POSITIVE** and stand with **GOD**, then you must not join NEGATIVE AND EVIL politics. Because you cannot speak, exactly what you want to do as a politician and that is not conducive to the way of **GOD**, because, as soon as you make a statement, it shall come to pass. When you twist and joke with the **WORD**, you disrespect the **WORD**. All lawyers are disrespect the

Conqueror, Cover and The signature

WORD, and many politicians also disrespect that **WORD**, and that is why these professions and the **TRUTH** and **GOD** cannot be friends.

Being lawyer can be a very **GOOD** profession. **I THE FATHER GOD** knows that it can be a very **GOOD** profession to be lawyer, because they can bring things into the **LIGHT** and can do many things, but they are twisting the **WORD**. They toy and mingle with **THE WORD** and are **WORD** con-fusionist, therefore they show official disrespect to the **WORD**.

Lawyers and politicians show disrespect to the **WORD**, but if you are a king or in any kind of office you should have the principle that you stand by the **WORD** that you utter by not altering the **WORD** at another opportunity. And that is the two different **SIGNATURES** that you want. It is either you twist and joke with the **WORD** and the **WORD** **APPROVES** what you want for you

Conqueror, Cover and The signature

temporarily without the **SIGNATURE** of the **TRUTH** or you accept to **SPEAK** what you have in mind and believe that it will stand with the **SIGNATURE** which is the **TRUTH**.

I have now explained that the **STAMP** is the idea in that when you start thinking, you have carved something but not yet sought **APPROVAL**, but as soon as you **SPEAK**, the **WORD**, that is the **APPROVAL**, because you have vocalised it, therefore it must come to pass. However coming to pass depends on whether it is negative or **POSITIVE**. Now that every human being understands this, you will think well about what you have in your heart, before saying it. You have to **THINK WELL**, before you can **SPEAK WELL**, because when you do not think well, you cannot speak well. When you **THINK WELL** and **SPEAK WELL** then the **TRUTH** will **SIGN** what you have put in place. **MY APPROVAL** is when you utter a

WORD and **MY STAMP** is when you have a **THOUGHT** as an idea.

D: **MY SIGNATURE**

MY SIGNATURE is the **TRUTH**. The **TRUE SELF** of the whole matter in-between this point will be known and that is when we would all know what type of **WORD** you **SPEAK**. How do you respect and value the **WORD** when you **SPEAK** what you do not mean? All the people that think well of the world and want to keep the world in **PEACE** are the people that **SPEAK** the **TRUTH** all the time in their life. **A TRUTHFUL** judge will deliver a **TRUE** judgement. **A TRUTHFUL** lawyer or a **TRUTHFUL** preacher or any profession that uses the **WORD** to instruct and work should **DELIVER** a **TRUE** message, before you can have the divine **SIGNATURE** of **THE FATHER GOD** attached to that **WORD**. This is the difference between an empty **APPROVAL** and **APPROVAL** with the

Conqueror, Cover and The signature

SIGNATURE of **GOD**. **MY SIGNATURE** is the **HOLY SPIRIT OF TRUTH**. The **HOLY SPIRIT OF TRUTH** divines the **WORD** and takes the **WORD** that is **TRUE** and **POSITIVE**.

Every **TRUTHFUL WORD** is **POSITIVE** and has **MY SIGNATURE**, but no idol **WORD** which is negative has **MY SIGNATURE** attached. That means that you are the one that signed it, and that is falsification of **MY SIGNATURE**. If you know in your heart that you are not **TRUTHFUL** as lawyers and politicians, **I** repeat, because the two of them are working together then you do not have **MY SIGNATURE**. When **I** talk about lawyers, **I** mean the untruthful ones if there is such a thing as a **TRUTHFUL** lawyer. Or if there is such a thing as a **TRUTHFUL** politician, but **I** think that there is. A politician that does what he or she says is a **TRUTHFUL** politician. If you are a lawyer that can present the case as exactly what you know to be the **TRUTH** then you can be a **TRUTHFUL** lawyer. However, if you twist the **WORD** to suit you so that you will win the case or you tell people that you will give them a road when you will not even give them a street, then you are not **TRUTHFUL** to yourself, and you have falsified **THE FATHER GOD'S SIGNATURE** to get what you want. And you get a failed **APPROVAL**. Everybody knows that it is the **SPOKEN WORD** that they use to gain an advantage in a situation in everything.

You must **SPEAK** to get what you want. You **SPEAK** to your wife, you **SPEAK** to your children, you **SPEAK** to your congregation, and you **SPEAK** to the public and to everyone that you have to talk with. No matter what happens, you use the **SPOKEN WORD** to do everything. Satan himself uses the **WORD** to do everything. Satan falsifies **THE FATHER'S SIGNATURE** for everything connected to negativism. Satan is called the master forger, because everything that Satan says is negative, false and a lie therefore; he is an international and universal forger for not being **TRUTHFUL**.

You should believe from the day that you have this Revelation Lecture that you are forging **THE FATHER'S SIGNATURE every** time that you **SPEAK** what is not **TRUE**. You force an event to take place such as putting someone in a post, when you know full well that the person is not doing well. You cognize with people to accept that person thereby forging **GOD'S SIGNATURE** and depriving the **TRUTH** to come to pass, then you are fighting against the natural **SUPREME SIGNATURE** of **THE FATHER GOD ALMIGHTY**, which is the **TRUTH**. Be you a president, a governor, a preacher, a lawyer, a king, a child, a woman, a man, an adult or any position as a spirit, angel, Jehovah or God that thinks that you have power to use falsehood to implement something and say that you have conquered, know from today that, you are revealing yourself in your heart as a forger. You have forged the **SIGNATURE** of **THE FATHER GOD** and you all know what it is means when you forge someone's **SIGNATURE**. **I AM** revealing **MYSELF** in a quite way. **I** know that a lot of people will hate **THE FATHER'S TALK** (**GOD PRESENT**) because they are forgers. And as soon as you hear this Lecture Revelation and you are not happy in your heart, and then know that, you are forging your heart against this **WORD** therefore; your judgement starts immediately in your heart from that point.

You gang against someone in your work place, because you are a manager, you are a president and you bigger than that person is. Therefore, you deprive that person and you know that what you are doing is not **TRUE** then you are forging the **SIGNATURE** of **THE FATHER GOD.** You must know that **LIGHT** stands for the **TRUTH**, and The **WORD** is **TRUTH**, **GOD** stands for the **TRUTH** and **LIGHT** means **TRUTH** and, the **TRUTH** means **LOVE**. The **TRUTH** means **KINDNESS**, **MERCY**, and all the **GOOD** things that make the world to be **GOOD**, therefore why should some people, deprive other people their privilege? If you deprive another person, his or her natural privilege because you are a politician or in any position through the spirit or physically, then you are forging the **SIGNATURE** of **GOD**, because you do not stand under the **TRUTH** to do what you do and **MY SIGNATURE** is **TRUTH**.

The **TRUTH** is in everyone's heart, because only you know the **TRUTH** about yourself. It is only you that knows the **TRUTH** of what you think and what you plan, because **TRUTH** is in everybody heart. Since you continue to do what you want to do, because you put your feet down, and stamp feet thinking that you have succeeded by prayer then know that you will pay for it. If it is by fasting or by going to meet a soothsayer or a big person, an officer, or through any other assignment in any form to falsely implement something to happen, know that you and your group of forgers will pay for it. **I THE SUPREME NATURE, THE SUPREME WORD, THE FATHER GOD** will ask you to pay and you will face the consequence of forging **MY SIGNATURE** and depriving the **TRUTH** from happening.

This is the Revelation Lecture that **I** want all creation to know about so that when you go about cognizing against someone saying that majority carries the vote, know that, yes it is a majority, but a majority of forgers. The majority that cognize against a widow, a poor person a lonely person as someone that has no one, however **THE FATHER GOD** is everything for that person, yet you vote against the truth to conquer that person and think that you will not face the consequence? You cognize against someone that is an illiterate and does not know much or a woman who does not have much power and think that you will not face the consequence for standing against such a person? All the negative people in the world have come together to promote elementary spirits, such as witchcraft among other sorts of negative spirits, and because they are so many they think that they have succeed. They are all called the group of forgers of evil. **MY SIGNATURE OF TRUTH** is not there, because you have signed it for yourself.

You know in your heart that you are negative, therefore, you force the situation and by so doing you deprive others their portion of things, suppress them and deprive their rights. Evil people want to have plenty of money because they cannot rule by **TRUTH**. They ensure that there are many hungry people around, so that when they give small amounts of money, the hungry people will bow down for them. You, the evil person that spreads money around for hungry people and then gives them knives and weapons to go and fight against innocent people, and deprive them of their rights. You will pay for it, because you are a forger of **GODS SIGNATURE** which is the **TRUTH**. You know that the position that you inherit belongs to someone else, and what you are doing is wrong, but you refuse to accept **THE FATHER GOD'S SIGNATURE** which is **TRUTH**. Rather you use your position, your 'big man and position', your tradition, your tripe or congregation and any magnitude that you have spiritually or physically to deprive the rightful people.

You do this because you have joined witchcraft and secret societies to command and invoke with your group, and do anything to get to where you are. However, know from today that although you have done that and succeeded in your own way, by forging the **TRUTH**, the **TRUE** position in your heart still remains and you cannot escape from that. You deprive the **TRUTH**, and deny the **TRUTH**, but what about the **TRUE** position in your heart that you cannot change or **ESCAPE**? That will become your judgement.

Today, **I** have proved **MY LOVE** to humankind by bringing out this hidden **WISDOM** and hidden **UNDERSTANDING** to you in case you did not know. **I** want this information to spread all over the world. It does not matter whether you believe in **GOD** or not or if you are a **GODLY** person.

This is about **TRUTH** and falsehood. Falsehood means that you have forged the **SIGNATURE** of **THE FATHER GOD**, because the

Conqueror, Cover and The signature

SUPREME NATURE'S SIGNATURE is **TRUTH** and anything that works without the complete concept of **TRUTH** means that you have forged the position and the situation.

If you forge something and it happens for you, it can only be temporal, because **I THE SUPREME SIGNATURE OF TRUTH** will arise and demand that you give up that position for the rightful person and that is when you will see the consequence of your actions. Even if you die, you will come back to pay for it. This is the situation that **I** want everyone to be aware of. It is either you stay wherever you are and mind you business, <u>stay hungry</u> and humble yourself and take what the **TRUTH** gives to you, because what belongs to you is the **TRUTH** with **THE FATHER GOD'S SIGNATURE** or you face the consequence for forgery.

Anything that comes to you by the **TRUTH** is merited by you as what you deserve and people will vote for you so that you will have it naturally, as **TRUTH**, then your conscience will be clear. If your conscience is clear with anything that you have, then that means that **THE FATHER'S SIGNATURE** is there with you and nothing will happen to you. Even if people fight and take it away from you, it does not mater, because those people are forgers and at the end of the day, it will come back to you as the rightful owner. This is what happened with Jacob and Esau. It happened that the **TRUE BLESSING** was for Esau, but because ESAU laboured much wanting to be **TRUTHFUL** to his father who he **LOVED**, he was always busy on errands for his father; therefore, he had no time to go to the kitchen. However, Jacob was a very, very lazy, but a handsome boy who was as fair as his mother was and because of that, his mother **LOVED** him. People always **LOVE** someone that is like them. Even if that person is evil they do not mind, as far as he or she is as evil as they are and resembles them, they **LOVE** that person because as it said, the birds of the same feather fly together. Nobody hates anyone that resembles him or her unless they are **TRUTHFUL**, and then they do not want people to get the same waiting punishment that is awaiting them.

As a result of the situation of Esau, the mother cognized with Jacob to deprive Esau of his blessing, but **I AM** telling you that all the people that came from that tribe are paying for it today, and you who laughs last, will laugh the best. All the people that suppress the suppressed will receive their due rewards and the suppressed are those who will win forever. Isaac knew that although Jacob felt like Esau when he touched him, he was not Esau because the voice was not that of Esau. It was only the body that was as Esau so when Esau came back he made a pronouncement and gave his **SIGNATURE** to Esau.

He told him that **I** know that your brother and you mother have connived to craftily deceive you and take your blessing, but at that end of the day, you will use my **SIGNATURE** to conquer. The whole world should wait and see how Africa which is Esau will take **SUPREME** place on this earth plane despite not knowing anything in the beginning. If you talk about technology, they backward, you talk about **LOVE**, they are backward, you talk about quality of life, they are backward, if you talk about so many things they are backward and they hate themselves, because they think that they are not very **GOOD**. However, **I AM** telling you today that the **ORIGINAL SIGNATURE** of the **TRUTH** is for them and that means that no matter what they are like, they will better, because every **GOOD** thing has returned back to them, *Amien*. And everybody will share with them, but they are the people that will cut the share and give to other people, because they have the **ORIGINAL SIGNATURE** of **THE FATHER GOD**.

Any country that uses *wayo, wayo, wayo* (cunning ways) to take things from other countries through craftiness and stealing by going about depriving other countries of what they have will pay for it. All the *wayo* countries that want to continue to be a rich country that everybody goes to knowing full well that the **TRUE SIGNATURE** is not with them then when they will pay back, theirs will be the worst. This is what all individuals, groups and governments should know. If you can be humble and accept this Lecture Revelation, then you will learn something that will benefit your soul. If you can stay where you are then you are better off, because if you use forcefulness to gain anything, when the **TRUE SIGNATURE** comes it would use the same power and take it away from you.

Conqueror, Cover and The signature

If for instance you use cunning to take someone's woman and you do not bother to ask and check well as to whether someone really loves that woman and the woman actually loves another man. But perhaps pressurise the woman with money or by other means to take the woman, then you will face the same situation and there are no two ways about it.

If you do anything and divert something for yourself even if is feast, the feast may still take place but the **TRUE SIGNATURE** is not there. As a result, the **TRUE** thing must come to super impose it and this is what **I** call the **TRUE** judgment of the **SUPREME NATURE** which is **MY SUPREME SIGNATURE**. Everything happens according to the **TRUE** and **ORIGINAL SIGNATURE** of **THE FATHER GOD**. Whatever you do on earth through your transit such as bribing angels, sacrificing, fasting or doing any assignment to get something that does not belong to you, you will vacate that position when the **ORIGINAL SIGNATURE** comes for the rightful owner to take over. This is because you have no **SEAL**, **RECEIPT** and **POWER** with that position.

Any forged **SIGNATURE** lacks something that only the **ORIGINAL** and **AUTHENTIC SIGNATURE** will have. You may say oh **GOD** has **APPROVED** something and that is why you have succeeded. It is only because you have **SPOKEN THE WORD** and **EVERY WORD** must come to pass so you are happy that you have it, but it is temporal. You have what you have, because of your money and position that you use to run around to cognize with people or use spiritual manipulation however there is no **SEAL**, therefore at the end of the day you are the looser.

When you read this Lecture Revelation, there are **TRUTHFUL** things in you heart, which **I THE FATHER GOD** will activate in you, that will help you to know more things that are connected to this Lecture Revelation whilst you are reading.

E: **MY SEAL**

Since you have no **TRUTHFUL SIGNATURE** on what you have, only a forged one, then there is no **ORIGINAL SEAL** on whatever that you think that you have. As there is no **SEAL**, it means that **I** did not **AUTHENTICATE** it. It is not just about having **MY SIGNATURE**. What is **MY SIGNATURE**?

MY SIGNATURE is **TRUTH**. Since you can **SPEAK** the **WORD**, you cognize with **THE WORD**, because the **WORD** is all and all. And that is why people say that **THE FATHER GOD** is everything, because everything is the **WORD**, Satan uses the **WORD**; **GOD** uses the **WORD** because the **WORD** means the

Conqueror, Cover and The signature

CREATOR of everything in the heaven and on earth. **I** have revealed that the tree in the Garden of Eden means the **WORD** that conceives both negative and **POSITIVE**. And when you eat that fruit, your eyes will open to know what is **GOOD** and what is bad and that is the **SPOKEN WORD**.

You can use the **WORD** to **SPEAK GOOD** and use the **WORD** to speak badly, but if you **SPEAK WELL** it is for you, and if you do not speak well, it is for you. **I** have now revealed the differences. The **WORD** means **APPROVAL**. You first **THINK** as the carving of the **STAMP** and bring it forward as a **SPOKEN WORD** then the **WORD APPROVES** it. However, what happens with **MY SIGNATURE**? Because when the idea takes effect and it is not the **TRUTH**, then **MY SIGNATURE** is not there and that means that you have forged it and that is the problem for you. And if **MY SEAL** is not there it means that **MY SIGNATURE** is not there because

MY SEAL is the **TRUTH** therefore, there are two different things. There is the one that Satan signs for you through your ulterior motive, cunning, craftiness, bribery, cognizing, evil power by making people to put it in place for you are the forged one. However, the **TRUTHFUL** one is the one that **I** have **SIGNED** and that means that anything that **I** give you, nobody can take it away from you, *Amien*. This is what it means.

For instance, **I** have talked about the first **POSITIVE** human being on earth as Abel after Adam. **I** told Abel to show appreciation so that **I** could see his mind because **I** wanted to **AUTHENTICATE** that he was **POSITIVE**, so that **I** could put **MY SEAL** and **MY SIGNATURE** for him. When Abel showed appreciation for **GOD,** he did so with a full heart. As a result, **I** have **SEALED** that every **APPRECIATION** to **GOD** must come through Abel and all the offspring as those who came from that **SEAL** must always be **TRUTHFUL**. They do not fear anything. Do you not see the way Cain killed Abel? Being killed is not a problem for **TRUTHFUL** people. If you kill them, it does not mean that you have killed the **TRUTH** or you take what belongs to them. (*Ha-ha*). If they die, they die, they take whatever belongs to them wherever, they go. When they come back, they come back with what is theirs.

    Do you not see King Solomon of Israel? After King Solomon, show **ME** any other King that can behave like him. He died with his blessing and his gift and that is why when Rehoboam his son came, he could not do much. If you go and kill any child of **THE FATHER GOD** and think that you have buried them, that is not the case rather, you are helping them to multiply more, because the **SEAL** means plentiful, abundance and the cock to crow. And that is why if you are clever, you will leave a **TRUTHFUL** person alone because, if you interfere with a **TRUTHFUL** person, you are in trouble. You know that **ALMIGHTY FATHER GOD IS TRUTH**, and you know that **I** have vowed that **I** will never **CHANGE** because **I AM UNCHANGEABLE** and **I** say that anything that **I** give to King Solomon, **I** will not take away and give to another person. Nobody, before and after him as Abel would have that blessing and he has come back to do this work now and nobody can deprive him of that. And since nobody can deprive King Solomon, the incarnate Abel of his blessing then that is it! For this reason, if you plan evil about a **TRUE** child of **GOD** with the **SEAL** of **GOD** on him or her you are in trouble. You will go naked on the street to confess, because you are a forger.

Do not forget that anything that has the **SEAL** of **THE FATHER GOD** on it stands forever, go to heaven and come back that is it! The **SEAL** means when **I THE FATHER GOD,**

THE SUPREME WORD STAMPS, APPROVES and **SANCTIFIES**, then that is it. When **MY SEAL** is not on something, then it is possible that, that thing is forged. Do you have the **SEAL** of **GOD** with the event that you want to bring about? Is there the **SEAL** of **GOD** in the **WORD** that you **SPEAK**, is in that is what you are saying a **TRUTHFUL WORD**? Do you have a **SEAL** for that position that you want?

Ask yourself these questions. When you use talisman to preach, or use talisman to conduct healing, does that have the **SEAL** of **GOD**? When you use deceit to get a position, does the position, have the **SEAL** of **GOD** on it? **GOD'S ORDINANCE** and **ORDINATION SPIRIT** is the **SEAL**. Anything that **GOD** gives you means, **HE** has **ORDAINED** you and that is the **CROWN**. **ORDAINED** by the **SEAL** of **GOD** means the **SPIRIT** of **CHRIST** is the **TRUTH**.

CHRIST means the King and anybody that **GOD ORDAINS, HE** gives the person the **SEAL** of **APPROVAL, STAMP** and **I** will **DELIVER** by **MYSELF**. If anything on this earth does not have **MY SEAL**, you will be able to know for yourself. When you see a situation which not **TRUTHFUL** or **POSITIVE**, then know that **MY SEAL** is not there and it means that it will not last. Any story, conduct, behaviour, position, action, and anything else in this world that does not have **MY SEAL** will not last.

Anything that you have in this world which is not based on the **TRUTH** means that there is no **SEAL** of **GOD** on it, because **GOD** means **TRUTH, HIS SIGNATURE** is **TRUTH** and **HIS SEAL** means that **I** have **APPROVED, STAMPED** and **SEALED** it. This means that **I** have **AUTHENTICATED** it in that the **WORD**, the position and the event is **TRUTHFUL** and it therefore comes from **ME THE FATHER GOD**

ALMIGHTY. Anything **TRUTHFUL** comes from the **POSITIVE** side of **GOD** and it would be everlasting. Whenever and wherever, it goes, it will still come back. **LIGHT** can never be quenched, and **LIGHT** is always **TRUTHFUL**, and the **TRUTH** is always **LIGHT**, and **LOVE** can never vanish. Anything that is based on **LOVE** is **TRUTHFUL**, and goes with **MERCY**, **PEACE**, **KINDNESS** and **HUMILITY**, and would last forever. A **PEACEFUL** person is always **GOOD**, because peace is from the family of the **TRUTH** as such from today **SIGN** up for this **TRUTH**. Sign up for the **SEAL** of **GOD**.

If you want anything, pray to **GOD** and do not struggle for anything in this world. You can pray to **GOD** for anything that you want, and if that thing is **GOOD** for you to have, and you wait then you will have it because your blessing will come from **THE FATHER GOD**, and not from human. Your riches come from **THE FATHER**

GOD and not from human. Nothing that will come to you naturally will come from anyone. It will be from **ME THE FATHER GOD**. Since **I** have **BLESSED** HRM King Solomon **ETE** with the **STAMP APPROVAL SEAL** and **SIGNED**, **I** will **DELIVER MY** assignment, **MY** mind, and **MY** mission with him and that is why you see all these Lecture Revelations upon Lecture Revelations. Even if it is only one lecture like this, it is enough that **I** have **DELIVERED** it through him to save mankind. You can even forget about any other thing and base everything you do on being **TRUTHFUL** in your entire life and accept the **SIGNATURE** of **THE FATHER GOD** as the **APPROVAL** of **THE FATHER GOD**, and that alone can mark you as a **TRUE** child of **GOD** and would save your soul and your life.

By basing your actions on the **TRUTH**, it means that you want every situation to come from **GOD** with the

APPROVAL and **SEAL** of **THE FATHER GOD** and that means that you are giving **RESPECT** to **GOD** by not forging his **SIGNATURE** in order to get what you want. You should not forge **MY SIGNATURE** for anything. Anything that you get by cognizing with others, by telling lies and doing anything untruthful, is an evil that you commit against **ME** as a forger. And there is no greater evil that you can commit against **PERSONALITY** than by forging their **SIGNATURE**.

There is nothing that you can do that will be more painful to **GOD** than to do what is not **TRUTHFUL**. That is what Lucifer did. There is no actual sin that Lucifer committed except to disagree with **ME** and when you disagree with **THE FATHER GOD**, with the **TRUTH** in your heart then you are an offspring of Lucifer. From today, know that the meaning of Satan is the same as the meaning of Lucifer which is falsehood. From this basis, know that anything you are doing that is untruthful means that it is Satan that is directing you, and you are forging **THE FATHER GOD'S SIGNATURE**. And any forger will pay a serious price, because that is the worst crime that you can commit against a **PERSONALITY**.

If you forge the **SIGNATURE** of king or president or anyone, you are trying to ruin the life of that person by suggesting that what you have is agreed by that person when it is not then you are looking for trouble.

All the people that do things that are not **TRUTHFUL** by telling lies and presenting them as the **TRUTH**, turning black to be white through the **WORD**, planning against the **WORD**, manipulating and twisting the **WORD** by doing what you like with the **SPOKEN WORD** which is **ME** are looking for **MY** trouble. And the consequence that you will face would be immeasurable. This is the message that **I** can give to you, **MY** dear humankind children on earth.

You should check yourself and ensure that you are not crashing with the **DIVINE BEING** called, **THE FATHER GOD THE CREATOR OF THE UNIVERSE** by forging every situation through lies. You are trying to prove that **THE FATHER GOD** has accepted what **I** have not accepted and you do, because of that your conscience would never be correct unless you stop your forgery. This is **MY SEAL**.

F: MY DELIVERY AGENT

So far are the **STAMP, APPROVAL, SIGNATORY, SEAL** and **DELIVERED**! Who **DELIVERS MY ORDERS**? It is an angel as **ME** in the dual mode.

Anything that **I SIGN** and **SEAL** must be **DELIVERED** for eternity without any hindrance and that is why when you struggle for something and it does not work, you should relax because it means that **THE FATHER GOD** has not **APPROVED** it. And do not accept anything that involves craftiness and forcefulness, because that is not your **TRUE POSITION**, the **TRUE** thing. Anything that is **TRUTHFUL** will come to you in a wonderful way.

Do you not realize that when Absalom fought to take the throne of his father King David, when originally the one to be in the throne had already being born called King Solomon, he was not able to succeed rather he died. How could Solomon fight for that position when he was a small child? Indeed, he could not fight and he did not go to war, because his **FATHER GOD** had fought all wars for him.

Any position that **I** keep for you will not have any opponent to struggle with you. And fighting, struggling and killing your-self for position of anything is from satanic doctrine. This is the reason that **I** do not like negative and evil politics. However, there is something that **I** will do about it. Satan has established it for the sons of men to create enemies in the whole world, because evil people knew that with **HUMILITY** and **ACCEPTANCE** a king will be born. And that king will be born with the **SEAL** and **APPROVAL** as **ORDAINED** by **THE FATHER GOD** to come and rule with **HUMILITY** and a **QUALITY** of **LOVE** with other **QUALITIES** of rulership. If you check any natural king that has been sent by **GOD** to rule, they will have the **QUALITIES** of rulership even if they are a child or a woman. They will have **QUALITIES** of **PEACE**, of **HUMILITY**, of **LOYALTY**, of **MERCY** and **TRUTH** will be the watch **WORD**, and everything that you can think of from **THE FATHER GOD** will be in that person because that person has come via **GOD THE SUPREME LOVE** and o**rdained** by **GOD**. And this is the person that has the **SEAL**, **STAMP** and **APPROVAL** with **MY SIGNATURE**, and he or she would **DELIVER**.

Why do you go to people so that you will win an election with money by campaigning and twisting the **WORD**? And most of the people involved in this behaviour are lawyers. How will you find **TRUTH** in such a situation? People have already made a lot of money to use to fight. Each politician has access to money and they steal a lot of money to keep. Do you know why they steal so much money, especially in Africa? They steal money to use to manipulate the election and create gangs for campaigning and when they eventually have the power and a lot of money, then the **TRUTH** will not prevail again and that is why you will not see a **TRUTHFUL** person that leads. All the people that are **TRUTHFUL** back off and squat in the bush, because they do not like trouble.

A **TRUTHFUL** person does not like trouble. Whom are you going to challenge and fight with? When **I** chose King David to be a King of Israel, he was nobody to be known and he was not even the first son of Jesse. People say that the first son must always rule? Who told you this? What if the first son is not born as a king, how will he rule? Supposing he has no **PEACE**, no **LOVE**, no manners, and cannot think twice and be steady then how can he rule. Some people say that a woman cannot rule but what if the woman has **LOVE**, she has **PEACE** and is born as a queen then she can rule and manage; and that is why there is no law in the **TRUTH**. The **TRUTH** means that the **SEAL**, **APPROVAL** and **DELIVERY** is inbuilt into a person that is born from **GOD** to come and do a particularly assignment. It does not matter whether such a person is a child, woman or a man or whether he or she is the first, middle or last born. When you want to choose someone, check the qualities that you will need for that job.

If you are a **TRUTHFUL** president, look for ministers and governors that have qualities that will suit the plan that your government has as a positive government. And the plan that you have for the country but of course, if you are a president that plans to dupe the government then you put people in place that will follow you to dupe the country. If you are a governor that is **TRUTHFUL** then you will look for and put in place all the local government chairpersons that will sign up to your **TRUTHFUL** character and administration. However, when you are not **TRUTHFUL**, you always look for the people that will hide under you to steal. The same thing goes to the councillors. In a church, a dubious preacher likes dubious elders and people that will cognize with him to share the church money. However if you are a **TRUTHFUL** person, they will not like you because any **TRUTHFUL** person is always a threat to a bad community and a bad gang of untruthful people.

Why did people hate **OUR LORD JESUS CHRIST**? It is because **HE** was **TRUTHFUL** and very vocal. The same thing applied to John the Baptist. Anyone that is vocal and **SPEAKS** the **TRUTH** is not liked by the world. It did not start today however today, **I** have revealed the spirit of **THE FATHER GOD** and how **THE FATHER GOD** sends people that come to help other people.

How will you have **PEACE** on earth when you chose the wrong people to lead you? You suppress the **NATURAL** rulers, the natural kings, and natural ruler-ship and chose untruthful people because of your gangs. When those who are in positions of leadership are from secret societies called 'oponi', freemasons, lords and Rosicrucian among others, they will put all their members to rule. Even in the church and other places of worship, you will always put the members of that church to be in important positions irrespective of whether they have the qualities needed for that position. And because you only choose members, those who have negative plans against you will say 'oh so these people only chose their members' and as a result, they will come and join your church or organisation. From there they become members and that is how they will have access to positions of authority that would lead to your downfall.

If you are **TRUTHFUL** and spirited then you will not use the idea of church members or any other members to choose those you place in important positions. You should not be led by the fact that someone is in your group rather you choose the type of person that will **DELIVER** what **GOD** has given to the community if you are **TRUTHFUL** person.

This book is another **MANUAL OF LIFE**. This Lecture Revelation is an **EYE OPENER** for every soul to use to change things in order to make things **WELL** in the world if you are **TRUTHFUL**. **THE FATHER GOD'S SIGNATURE** is required in any position that you hold, therefore if you have this **SIGNATURE** in your hand, you will succeed in your life. **MY SIGNATURE** is **TRUTH**. Be **TRUTHFUL** and **I** will stand on your side to **SIGN, SEAL** and **DELIVER** for you. And **I** promise you that **I** will never leave any **TRUTHFUL** person half way *IN THE NAME AND THE BLOOD OF OUR LORD JESUS CHRIST*, *Amien*.

I will always **SIGN** and **SEAL** and **DELIVER** even before they are born and **I** will know them, **I** will know how many years that they will spend on this earth, and how well they will do because, **I AM TRUTH** in them. **I** in them **AM** the **TRUTH,** because **I** built them for **TRUTH**, and **I** will always be with them. Do not attempt to fight them, because you will never succeed. Instead of you to succeed, **I** will bulldoze you out. If you see anything happen to any child of **GOD**, know that it is the will of **THE FATHER GOD**. When **JESUS CHRIST** died, it was not the Jews that killed him; it was the will of **THE FATHER GOD** that he should die for the sins of man there do not go being proud that you have successfully harmed a child of **GOD** unless he or she is not a **TRUTHFUL** person.

TRUTH is **POWER**, **TRUTH** is the **MANTLE**, and **TRUTH** is more than a bomb. The **TRUTH** is more **POWERFUL** than anything in this world is, because the **SUPREME GOD OF CREATION** stands with the **TRUTH**. When you are **TRUTHFUL**,

THE HOLY SPIRIT OF TRUTH always stands with you, because that is the **SIGN**, **SEAL** and the **DELIVERY** of **GOD** in you. You are a sign of **FATHER GOD PRESENT** when you are **TRUTHFUL** in your spirit, and that is why when the **SPIRIT OF TRUTH** is with anyone, that person represents **FATHER GOD** as **GOD PRESENT**. From today, **I** want every soul on earth to **SIGN** for the **TRUTH**. You should use the **TRUTH** for anything that **GOD** sends you to do **I** will be with you. If you practice the **WORD** of this Lecture Revelation, the whole world will change overnight. And all Satanic and evil life will cease, because that is temporal.

Whatever you are that is based on lies can be scattered easily even if you have been in that position for a hundred years, because it is not **TRUE** and as a result, there is no **SIGNATURE** of **GOD** on it. **I** will be the agent that **DELIVERS** every situation of a **TRUTHFUL** person.

Conqueror, Cover and The signature

And any **TRUTHFUL** person that has access to this Lecture Revelation from today should have **PEACE** in mind and relax and continue to be on the side of **TRUTH**, because **I** will never leave you comfortless since you have the **SEAL** of **GOD** in you in the name of **OUR LORD JESUS CHRIST**, *Amien*.

G: **TICKING RIGHT**, **WRONG OR**, **ZAOF**

ZAOF is the opposite negative of **RIGHT** and means something that does not exist, because it is condemned. Whenever **I** say **ZAOF** and **TICK RIGHT** it means **I** create a demarcation between the two things. **ZAOF** means that something is false and when **I TICK RIGHT** it means that **I** have **APPROVED**, and **STAMPED** and **SEALED**. Do not rush for something when you see a **STAMP** on something. Do you see a **SIGNATURE** on it? Unless there is a **SIGNATURE** attached, you can not be certain of that thing. **I** have now revealed that the first thing is the **STAMP** which means that you have conceived a **THOUGHT**, be it **GOOD** or bad. You can think that something has been **APPROVED**, but there is a small mark that **I** would make on that thing to show **APPROVAL**, without which, forget about it because **MY SIGNATURE** is not there. People can forge other peoples **SIGNATURES**, but they cannot forge the **SEAL**. It is only the **SEAL** that will make all angels and **MY SPIRITUAL SELF** to stand by you for whatever you want to do. However, the **SIGNATURE** is the **SPOKEN WORD** that can be forged by Satan.

Do you know that there are so many angels that **I** send to this world, but because of the cunning things of this world, they join people here. There are so many spirits souls that come from water and join human beings, and there are also so many aliens that come and bully things on earth and you think that it is **GOD** that is doing it. People tend to think that very fair and white individuals are angels and Black people are Satan. It does not work like that. It works through the **TRUTH**. It is only through the **TRUTH** that you will know when **I THE FATHER GOD APPROVES** something. **TRUTH** is the sign of **GOD** and that is the **SIGNATURE of THE FATHER GOD THE CREATOR OF THE UNIVERSE**. When **I** mark anything **ZAOF**, know that it is condemned and **MY** hand is not there. However, when **I TICK RIGHT**, it means that **I AM** solidly there with an **AUTHENTIC SEAL** to ensure that whatever and whoever is in place, should carry on for eternity., and no one can take such a thing away for the whom **I** have **SEALED**, in the name of **OUR LORD JESUS CHRIST**, *Amien*.

CONCLUSION A: **MY APPROVAL IS THE SPIRIT OF FULFILMENT.**

Whenever you can see that everything has been **FULFILLED** from spirit to soul and from soul to the physical body then know that all is well. The **FULFILMENT** is not what you feel physically, the **FULFILMENT** is in your **THOUGHT** and your **CONSCIENCE**. It is not something that after you have done it, you later say to yourself that 'what you have acquired does not belong to you, and that you only got it because you struggled for it. Or you say to yourself that you bought the position you have'. Or sit and ponder saying 'I forced this my wife that she should marry me, I know that she does not really **LOVE** me and the wife says this husband of mine, I only married him because of money, I do not really like him'. And all this means that, there is no **FULFILMENT** in your heart about what you have, because you have forged the situation. However, anything you have which has **LOVE** and **FULFILMENT** within yourself means that, **THE FATHER GOD APPROVES** it via your conscience.

CONCLUSION B: **EVERY WISH IS FOR THE PERSON THAT WISHES THE WISH**

EVERY WISH IS FOR THE PERSON THAT WISHES THE WISH. You may say that '**THE FATHER GOD** has **APPROVED** this and that for **ME**', are you sure? If you struggle and make someone to suffer by depriving them of what is theirs in the process of getting what you have, then what ever that you **WISH**, it **WISH** you, **WISH** you and that is the **SIGNATURE**. All humans should know that you can only take whatever you put in, and that is why **I** say that everyman shall reap what they sow.

Do not go about saying that **THE FATHER GOD** wants this and that to happen, and has **APPROVED** this and that. What did **I APPROVE**? It is because you have planed in you heart and **SPOKEN** a **WORD**. Even in the kingdom of **GOD** in heaven, **I** know what Lucifer and his gang are doing till today in the world all over. Whatever, they **WISH** is what will follow them. Anything that you **WISH** yourself and **WISH** for others will be the same thing that follows you. If you deprive people things, you are depriving yourself and if you help people to succeed, you help yourself to succeed. Try it and you will realize that, that is what is going on.

All the politicians that deprive others and enrich themselves will come back to be the poorest humans beings on this earth and **I** will make them to be under the people that they deprived. And that is what happens. This is what **I** told David. **I** said kneel down here at **MY** feet quietly with **HUMILITY** and **I** will make all your enemies to become your foot stool.

Do you not know that all the people in your nation, country, state, community, and village have equal rights to what you are using as a politician, a king, a queen, a president, a governor or any other type of leader? You should know that every national purse belongs to every citizen of the nation, but how much do you take and how much do you give to others. Do you do things equally for everybody? Since you have not done that, you are a debtor to the entire nation where you come from.

I THE FATHER GOD is the nature as **GOD** of **LIGHT**, **GOD** of **LOVE** and **I** have sent you to be a politician, a governor, a senator, a prime minister, a president, a local government chairman, a councillor, a village head and any senior post that you may have so that you can link with others to serve. However, you decide to deprive others and enrich yourself. When you do this, you are signing a voluntary evolution to poverty, in this life and others to come. And this is because in your

Conqueror, Cover and The signature

heart; none that you do are **TRUTHFUL**.

You deprive other people, because you have signed up to evil. You are in the secret society of evil and you think that it ends there. No, it does not end there, but it will end in your heart when you will die and be transferred. No matter how long you live, you will leave what you have acquired on earth. And you will go with a guilty conscience knowing that you are an original forger of **THE FATHER GOD'S SIGNATURE**, because what you are doing, is not **TRUTHFUL**, therefore you must die with it. And you will hear this Lecture Revelation whether you like it or not, because your friend will tell and many other people will also tell you. However, since you have died with a guilty conscience, you conscience will take you to foot to press you down as you have pressed others. And that is the meaning by what you **WISH**,

WISH, follows who **WISH**, the **WISHED**.

CONCLUSION C: EVENTUALLY YOU WILL GET WHAT YOU WANT

You know that you can transfer things to another place and then go and collect it there and that is what is happening in life. Everything that you do here, you will get it back. **I** will give you a short story before **I** end this Lecture Revelation.

There was once a Bishop who owned a church and this bishop had some servants and preachers so he always stayed at home as a big man. People always took food and donated for him. Everything is bishop, bishop and bishop. When they have to do any work in the community, he sends other members to do everything. He never helps anyone. Everyday, women take eggs for bishop and they take firewood for bishop. Everyone did everything for bishop so his wife

Conqueror, Cover and The signature

and children also did not do anything. Bishop oh, bishop oh, people would say. You know how important that status of bishop is. Bishop continues to stay at home not doing, anything. No work, no charity and no nothing. Even the poor people in the congregation had to donate to bishop so that bishop will bless them because before you can go and see the bishop, you must carry something, as you cannot go empty handed. And in fact, it is difficult to see bishop when you are not very rich. Just like all the big people in the church that you cannot see unless you are very rich. You can only see their members.

One night **GOD** sent an angel to assess bishop just as **GOD** sends angels to assess everyone. In this world, **I, THE FATHER GOD** always send angels to assess people so that they can bring your physical record, which **I** will compare with the spiritual one to see whether they tally together. During this assessment, you can dove off and dream and anything can happen, because of the spirit that is around you and this is what happened to the bishop. The angel put him into a dream mode. The bishop dreamed that he had died and when he died, 'they' took him to give his quarter in the other side. After seventy two hours of death, you will have to go to the central office of administration to rearrange for how long you are going to spend in the soul world before you can come back to this world to work again, if you are entitled to come back again. If not, then you will be kept there depending on the decision of the central administrators.

ENYE ODUDU!

The bishop taken on a long journey, because when people die their soul is taken back to their origin where their original home is. It does not matter whether you are born in Africa, in Europe, in America or any where else or if you are Black or White. Everybody goes to his or her original home where the head quarter of administration is, and from there, you can be sent anywhere. If you are from a Black home, but you were born as a White person, as soon as you die you will be returned to your original Black home, and that is how it works.

Anyhow, let's resume with the story of the bishop. When he went back to his community, he saw that there were many houses. Some were quarters with gardens, some were seven story buildings with all amenities and others were simple flats. When he passed one of the houses, he saw one of his servants that had died some years ago. He saw that his servant was in one of the seven story buildings with a big garden with so many people working under him. The servant came and said to the bishop, oh my master you have come? When he saw his servant he did not even want to greet him

Conqueror, Cover and The signature

however, he said to himself that if his servant can live in that type of house then his would be a palace as a hundred story building pad. He was taken pass the three story building area and pass the one floor buildings and then pass the bungalows and pass the road track to where people go to toilet. And in this area, there was a red thatched house that had some parts with holes in the ceiling where rain fell through. At this point, they told bishop that this was his house. He replied that they were crazy and that this could not be his house. They told him that those eggs are the empty baskets of all the eggs that he ate on the other side therefore, there was nothing left for him to use here. Bishop said that this could not be right and that they should return back to the office.

When they got to the office, they asked him his name and he said that he was Bishop so, so and so. They looked for the file of the bishop for a period longer than the time it has taken to give this Lecture Revelation but they could not find the file of the bishop. They looked everywhere until eventually they found it very far away when the bishop last did something whilst he was training to be a bishop and used to go on a few errands for people, but once he completed his training and became a bishop, he did not work again. And since he did not work, his file was dusty and was among the last files hidden away.

When they opened his file they told him that he has not paid any tithe, he has not helped anyone and was actually a debtor as such, he had to work to pay it off. They said that it would take him a number of years before he could come back and continue his life. The bishop started to cry and he cried so much that he asked if he could go back, but they refused. However, fortunately for him this was a dream, so when bishop woke up and opened his eyes, he was still in the physical world. And on that very day, there was an announcement that people should go and clean the church. Bishop carried a shovel and a broom and was the first person that arrived in the church. People said as usual 'oh bishop do not do anything'. He replied that they should leave him and in fact, everyone should rest because he would do everything on that day. Everybody was surprised. They said 'what happened to our bishop'? On Sunday, bishop was the first person to donate hundreds of pounds for **GOD**.

Bishop established charities and started saying that he was no longer a bishop and that everybody else was the bishop, rather, he was just a servant of **GOD**. Alleluia, Hallelujah! From that moment onwards bishop changed because he had seen 'jhajhakentek' (big trouble) because **GOD LOVED** bishop. That is what is happening to you. If you read this Lecture Revelation and ignore it trying to prove that, you know better then at some point, you will regret your decision. Do you know who talks like this? It is only **THE SPIRIT OF TRUTH** that can talk like this.

I brought this story and this Lecture Revelation so that you can help your soul. And if you want to help your soul, then change the way you **THINK** and your **CHARACTER** and **SIGN** up for the **TRUTH** and get the **SIGNATURE** and **SEAL** of **THE FATHER GOD** as the **SIGNATURE** of **TRUTH** in everything that you do. If you work with people that do not like the **TRUTH**, leave that place and **GOD** will not disappoint you. Do not join gangs to suppress and deprive people because your scenario would be worse than that of the bishop, if you do not change.

Let **MY PEACE** and **BLESSING** abide with the entire world now and forever, more, *Amien*.

Conqueror, Cover and The signature

ENYE ODUDU ABASI MI ZIM ZIM ZIM ASSASSU, POSITIVE, POSITIVE and POSITIVE.

In the Name of Our Lord Jesus Christ
In the Blood of Our Lord Jesus Christ
Now and forever more,

THANK YOU FATHER

Prayer by HRM Queen Disem Solomon David **ETE**

Let thanks and praises be given to **THE FATHER GOD** in the name of Our Lord Jesus Christ, Amien.

Let thanks and praises be given to **THE FATHER GOD** in the blood of Our Lord Jesus Christ, Amien.

Let thanks and praises be ascribed to the **ORIGINAL SIGNATORY**, the **ONE** who **SIGNS** and **SEALS** and **DELIVERS** even now and forever, more, Amien.

HOLY, HOLY, HOLY FATHER
Thank **YOU FATHER** for this recondite **WISDOM** which you have brought from thy recondite **LOVE** for humankind on this day, the celebration season of King David and Solomon anniversary week celebration of thanking **THE FATHER GOD**. Thank **YOU FATHER GOD** that trough this lecture, you have **SIGNED** and **SEALED** all **POSITIVE BLESSING** for all **POSITIVE** children of **GOD**. Thank

Conqueror, Cover and The signature

YOU FATHER GOD for the ability to sow well so that we may reap well because **YOU** have made us to know that nobody plants cassava and reaps banana, '**NO WAY**'! For this reason thank **YOU FATHER GOD** that you have given us the ability to plant **LOVE, MERCY, KINDNESS, HARD WORK, PATIENCE** so that we may reap same. Thank **YOU FATHER GOD** for making us not be like the bishop in that story rather, may we resemble **YOU, THE SPIRIT** that works twenty four hours, as the **ORIGINAL HARDWORKING SPRIT**, that plants well and harvest well so that we may be with **THEE** when **YOU** harvest all **GOODNESS** and all will be well with us, now and forever, more, Amien.

Let thanks and praises be given to **THE FATHER GOD** in the name of Our Lord Jesus Christ, Amien.
Let thanks and praises be given to **THE FATHER GOD** in the blood of Our Lord Jesus Christ, Amien.

Let thanks and praises be given **THE SUPREME SPIRIT OF TRUTH**, which is **THE SIGNATURE OF THE FATHER GOD THE CREATOR OF THE UNIVERSE**. And may we all stand with **THE TRUTH** so they the **TRUTH** will always stand with more, Amien and forever, us, now.

THANK YOU FATHER

Chapter Four

THE INSPIRATIONAL WRITER

KING SOLOMON SPIRITUAL LIBRARY
THE GOD ENCYCLOPAEDIA WORD OF INFINITY

INSPIRATIONAL WRITERS AND READERS OF THE
FATHER'S TALK
(GOD PRESENT)
KING SOLOMON SPIRITUAL LIBRARY

In the name of our Lord Jesus Christ In the blood of our Lord Jesus Christ Now and forever more, Amen

(A) REFERENCING THE FATHER'S TALK (GOD PRESENT) IN KING SOLOMON SPIRITUAL LIBRARY

I know some people will inspire when you visit King Solomon Spiritual Library website or bookshop, and have access to any of **THE FATHER'S TALK (GOD PRESENT)** information through books, electronics, audio and otherwise and are inspired to write or produce any information through the knowledge that you have gained, you must not fail to reference **THE FATHER'S TALK (GOD PRESENT)** in **King Solomon Spiritual Library** as the such of your inspirations.

(B) THE WORD OF TRUTH AND THE HOLY SPIRIT PRINCIPLES

Since **THE FATHER'S TALK (GOD PRESENT)** is the direct information from **THE FATHER GOD ALMIGHTY HIMSELF,** all positive children of God can be, and will be inspired with this **WORD** because the Word of **THE**

FATHER GOD, THE CREATOR OF THE UNIVERSE is a Spiritual Case Study for all souls to improve to have self awareness and a Higherself Consciousness.

When you are inspired and you want to write, make sure that your ideas, principles and concepts base on the Holy Spirit of Truth without changing the ordinance of the **FATHER'S TALK (GOD PRESENT).**

(C) THERE SHALL BE CONSEQUENCES THAT WOULD FOLLOW THOSE WHO USE THE MEANING, THE CONCEPTS AND THE PRINCIPLES OF THE FATHER'S TALK (GOD PRESENT) FOR THE PURPOSES OF MISLEADING

Consequences shall follow those who use the meaning, the concepts and the principles of **THE FATHER'S TALK (GOD PRESENT)** for the purposes of misleading in any manner.

Any Human-God, human-animal, human-bird or human-fish who has access to **THE FATHER'S TALK (GOD PRESENT)** through any means, be it via books, electronics, audio and otherwise should know that those words are not the words of human beings. The words are transcribed, proofread and accepted by **THE FATHER GOD** as it comes from the **SUPREME STUDIO OF THE ALMIGHTY FATHER GOD HIMSELF,** via **King Solomon Spiritual Library.**

When the signal of the information alerts HRM King Solomon David Jesse Etteh from **THE FATHER** through the **COMPREHENSIVE MEMORY OF GOD** in him, at anytime in the day or at night and anywhere, whether on the road or any public place, he will take note of the title of the Revelation Lectures. Sometimes if the location is conducive, lectures can take place immediately. If the location is not conducive, **THE FATHER** fixes the time for the full lecture to take place. Most of the time, some of the lectures take about a week, a month or six months and so on, to deliver when **THE FATHER** brings it back from **HIS SUPREME MEMORY** to HRM King Solomon Etteh.

Take note that the information of **THE FATHER'S TALK (GOD PRESENT)** is not preaching, or the giving of sermons or shared discussion. **THE FATHER** calls it ***"LECTURE REVELATION"***, which is a Spiritual Case Study for mankind to improve and have the Higherself Consciousness about himself or herself and their creator.

For that reason, every human being that comes across any of this information of the **FATHER'S TALK (GOD PRESENT)** should treat it with utmost and absolute respect and reverence at all times.

HRM King Solomon David Jesse Etteh is not responsible for **THE FATHER'S TALK (GOD PRESENT)** but **GOD HIMSELF. THE ALMIGHTY FATHER** only uses him as a way through, just like a loud speaker from the radio or television receiver.

For this reason, HRM King Solomon David Jesse Etteh will not be held responsible by anyone who does not understand the contents, the concepts and the principles of **THE FATHER'S TALK (GOD PRESENT)** information in King Solomon Spiritual Library. He will not answer any questions or queries from spirit to soul and the physical truth in connection to the above from the lower mind individuals, persons or groups. However, if you are positive and you have love, you are humble, have patience and are peaceful and you want to know and understand more of any part of **THE FATHER'S TALK (GOD PRESENT); 'You should use fasting and prayer'** and or if anyone has any questions in good faith, he or she is free to write to HRM King Solomon and **THE FATHER** in him will respond. He will not, and there is no response to any questions, queries and anything negative with the craftiness of the evil minds of humankind.

That is why you should first read

THE FATHER GOD with **HIS SUPREME HOLY SPIRIT OF TRUTH** will bless all those who read and accept this information with good faith through the name and blood of our Lord Jesus Christ. Amen.

In the name of our Lord Jesus Christ In the blood of our Lord Jesus Christ Now and forever more, Amen

Conqueror, Cover and The signature

"THEUNISAL-SUREME SEACELION"
The Universal Supreme Season Celebration

=========

"THEUNI-SUREME WORA THECRO-THEUNISE"
The Universal Supreme Word Almighty
The Creator Of The Universe

====================

WWW.COME4WORD.COM

THE OFFICIAL SITE FOR

EVERLASTING UNIVERSAL ALL WORD

Conqueror, Cover and The signature

SEASON APPRECIATION CEREMONIAL PROGRAM

==========

THE UNIVERSAL SUPREME ALL WORD SEASON

CELEBRATION
(GOD PRESENT)
SOMETHING MORE THAN
GOLD
IN THE HEART OF ALL MEN IS THE
WORD

THE WORD IS THE MAKER, THE SOLE ADMINISTRATOR AND THE CREATOR OF THE UNIVERSE. THEREFORE, ALL MANKIND ON EARTH MUST APPRECIATE THE WORD IN ALL CAPACITIES FOREVER

FROM EVERY OA OF AO TO AO OF AO (1st OCTOBER TO 10th OCTOBER.) YEARLY IS THE UNIVERSAL SUPREME

ALL WORD SEASON

CELEBRATION TO APPRECIATE THE FATHER GOD ALMIGHTY

Conqueror, Cover and The signature

WORDWORDWWORDWORDWORDWORD

CELEBRATION!
CELEBRATION!!
CELEBRATION!!!

THE
UNIVERSAL
SUPREME
WORD

Conqueror, Cover and The signature

CELEBRATION OF ALL TIME

=======

THE ALMIGHTY FATHER GOD, THE CREATOR OF ALL

Conqueror, Cover and The signature

THINGS
BROTHERHOOD

ORGANISED BY
KING SOLOMON SPIRITUAL LIBRARY

=======

HRM KING SOLOMON DAVID JESSE ETE
INSPIRATIONAL HEAD

IN THE HONOUR OF THE FATHER GOD THE CREATOR OF THE UNIVERSE THE HOLY SPIRIT OF TRUTH AND THE KING OF KINGS AND THE LORD OF LORDS

==========

THANK YOU FATHERo

Conqueror, Cover and The signature

KING SOLOMON SPIRITUAL LIBRARY

THE GOD ENCYCLOPAEDIA WORD OF INFINITY

===========

King Solomon Spiritual Library, God Universal Information Centre Father's Talk (God Present)

WITH LOVE

Covered: This **BOOK,** e-book, software or software's, books, website, video, audio, idea or ideas, formula or formulas, manual or instruction manual.

... Hereby gives you a non-exclusive license to use the ... (THIS BOOK). Some of the word here is coded with the (WORD OF SUPER HOLY AND INTELLIGENCE FATHER GOD ALMIGHTY)

Title, ownership rights, and intellectual property rights in and to the Website, Books, E-book, Audios and Videos, Shops and Store – e-Stores, Fundraisings, Celebrations and the supreme word seasons Celebration formulas and arrangement, Positive Inspiration, Holy (Fata), FATHER GOD ALMIGHTY POSSESSING SPIRIT in thought, in words and in did, thinking well, speaking well, hearing well and doing well shall remain in me and in ... The BOOK is protected by international copyright.

FATHER'S TALK (GOD PRESENT)
The message in The Father's Talk (GOD PRESENT) does not challenge any authority either individuals, groups or

governments of any land or even any belief of any form. It is rather challenging the truth that is hidden from mankind. Therefore, any spirit, soul or physical human being who decides to challenge this truth shall have himself or herself to blame.

Key A
Any individual that reads any of The Father's Talk (GOD PRESENT) with faith; love and acceptance will experience immediate positive change in his or her life from spirit, soul to physical. If he or she accepts the message then he or she will be free from any evil.

Key B: **PEACE AND LOVE**
If you do not believe the contents of any of The Father's Talk (GOD PRESENT) it is possible through The Father's divine love and peace simply hands over your copy to a friend or somebody else that would like to keep a copy, or signing out from any of the website that connected to The Father's

Talk (GOD PRESENT) KING SOLOMON SPIRITUAL e-LIBRARY without any evil and negative comments and you are blessed and free.

========

FROM THE DESK OF INSPIRATIONAL HEAD

Fees, Prices and Donations; There is no refund on fees, price or donations since your fees price or donations are using as a charity contribution to do administration work of THE SUPREME WORD, So please kindly read this first before you decide to involves yourself in any of the under mention of HRM King Solomon David Jesse ETE universal Inspirational Businesses of (GOD PRESENT) in cash, kinds and otherwise.

I CAME FROM THE FATHER GOD, WITH THE FATHER GOD, AND BY THE FATHER GOD TO ESTABLISH THE FOLLOWING:

Therefore, all distributors and contributors of The Father's Talk (GOD PRESENT),

The Spiritual Advice, Healing and Counselling on General Live (The Universal Supreme Spiritual General Hospital), New Songs and Psalms of King David and Solomon, The Word of **GOD** Processing City in Ikot Okwo or e-City online, The Trinity Celebration, **"OUC FUND"**, The Universal Bank Account For All Creations, **"ERUFA"** ETE Royal Universal Family, **"THEUNISAL-SUREME SEACELION"** The Universal Supreme Word Season Celebration To Appreciates THE FATHER GOD ALMIGHTY **"THEUNI-SUREME WORA THECRO-THEUNISE" The Universal Supreme Word Almighty, THE CREATOR OF THE UNIVERSE** should attach this information to all readers, website visitors, distributors, affiliates person/group, celebrant and celebrations centres, supporters and promoters, members, workers and voluntary workers, Ete royal universal palace committee, governments and many other centres as an agreement. Please kindly know that I am not answering to any physical human except **PEACE, UNITY AND LOVE.**

"THEUNISAL-SUREME WORA THECRO-THEUNISE".

I AM IN THE STAGE OF SUPER HOLY AND INTELLIGENCE FATHER GOD POSITIVE MADNESS OF THE HOLY SPIRIT OF TRUTH,
ENYEN ODUDU ODUDU ODUDU ABASI MI OOO ZIM ZIM ZIM ASSASU, POSITIVE POSITIVE POSITIVE. UKEMEKE AKA IDIOK UNAM.
Let the peace and blessing of the Holy Father abide with everybody who corporate with this divine Father's Talk (GOD PRESENT

THANK YOU FATHER

BY
THE HOLY SPIRIT OF

THE FATHER GOD THROUGH HIS SERVANT
Senior Christ Servant
HRM King Solomon David Jesse ETE
Brotherhood of the
Cross and STAR
Eteroyal Universal family
Ikot Okwo The Great City of Refuge,
Ete Community
Ikot Abasi LGA-543001
Akwa Ibom State Nigeria-W/A
Tel. 08036693841
www.ksslibrary.com
Email: ksslibrary@eteroyalmail.com

READ AT LEAST SEVEN LECTURE'S REVELATIONS BEFORE YOU CAN MAKE ANY COMMENTS

Conqueror, Cover and The signature

**In the Name of Our Lord Jesus Christ
In the Blood of Our Lord Jesus Christ
Now and forever more**

Everybody should have access and read at least seven **FATHER'S TALK (GOD PRESENT)** Lecture's Revelations before you can make any comments about it. If you do not go through at least seven **FATHER'S TALK** lectures and you comment you may make mistakes. When you make mistakes your blood will be upon you because you would have taken voluntary evolution to misquote **THE FATHER GOD THE CREATOR OF THE UNIVERSE.** If however, you go through any seven of **THE FATHER'S TALK (GOD PRESENT)** – one of **THE FATHER'S TALK** stands for one Spirit of God, which means that **FATHER'S TALK GOD PRESENT** Lectures Revelation are witness by the Seven Spirits of God, which I use as the Seven Church of God and Seven days of the Week, Seven spirits of Creations in

one Supreme energy of **THE FATHER GOD, THE SPOKEN WORD.**
When you read seven **FATHER'S TALK** Lectures then, **I THE FATHER GOD** will reveal you as positive person. Then you will have a portion in **ME**. One of **THE FATHER'S TALK** will have a portion in you. Then you would know that this information came from **THE FATHER GOD.**
The Father's Talk God Present is not a mere talk from a man!
In the Name of Our Lord Jesus Christ
In the Blood of Our Lord Jesus Christ
Now and forever more
WWW.THEWORDCITY.COM
www.ksslibrary.com

THE UNIVERSAL SUPREME ACKNOWLEDGEMENT

'THE ONLY SOURCE AND REMEDY

TO END ALL HUMANITIES PROBLEMS'

Join me to Celebrate;
Acknowledge,
Appreciates and give full RECOGNITION to
THE UNIVERSAL SUPREME WORD,
YOUR LIFE FORCE,
THE TOTALITY OF ALL TOTALITIES
YOUR CREATOR,
THE FATHER GOD ALMIGHTY,
THE CREATOR OF THE UNIVERSE

WWW.COME4WORD.COM
Contact EMAIL:
hrmkingsolomon@eteroyalmail.com

Conqueror, Cover and The signature

THANK YOU FATHER

Conqueror, Cover and The signature

ESTABLISH MY SPIRITUAL LIBRARY

I THE FATHER GOD ALMIGHTY THE SUPREME WORD OF THE UNIVERSE AM THE SPIRITUAL FOOD TO FEED YOUR SOUL. Therefore, **I** want every family in this world, every home in this world, every office, government offices, monarchies, countries, states, regions, counties, communities, local authorities compound, family homes, everyone everywhere should be collecting published copies of **THE EVERLASTING GOSPEL AND THE FATHER'S TALK (GOD PRESENT)** Lectures Revelations of KING SOLOMON SPIRITUAL LIBRARY should be established physically in your houses. So that everybody should have those RECORDS. Go to read the books regularly. Every family should have this Library **MY**

INFORMATION CENTRE for their family members.

Every generation of the particular family could easily go to their family Library of KING SOLOMON SPIRITUAL LIBRARY EVERLASTING GOSPEL and the **FATHER'S TALK (GOD PRESENT) Lectures Revelations** and read the Gospels and Lectures Revelations. Generations upon generations will access their KING SOLOMON SPIRITUAL LIBRARY.

You must all have **THE LIBRARY OF THE FATHER GOD ALMIGHTY** called **KING SOLOMON SPIRITUAL LIBRARY FATHER'S TALK (GOD PRESENT) LECTURES REVELATIONS** in your homes and offices. The authorities and individuals concerned must see to that. When you establish your branch of KING SOLOMON SPIRITUAL LIBRARY and have Everlasting Gospels and the **FATHER'S TALK (GOD PRESENT)** Lectures Revelations that place is blessed

Conqueror, Cover and The signature

and secured. In the name and Blood of Our Lord Jesus Christ, now and forever more, Amen.

THANK YOU FATHER

Conqueror, Cover and The signature

The title List of some of the

Father's Talk
(GOD Present)

1: THE MANUAL OF THE SPOKEN WORD

2: THE MANUAL OF LIFE

3: INVESTMENT WITH GOD

4: ISO IBOT EDEM IBOT

5: THE CHARACTER OF THE NEW WORLD

6: HELPMANTRANS

7: UNDERSTANDING MY WORD

8: TRUTH, POSITION, POST AND NAME

9: NON STOP BLESSING

10: IMPRESSION

11: STAGES OF EDUCATIONS (SPE, SSE & SUE)

12: THE ENGINEERING OF LIFE
13: THE CONTENT PACKAGE

14: THE BUDGET OF THE NEW WORLD

15: DIVINE ATTENTION

16: THE BABY SPIRIT

17: PROMOTION

18: ADVANCE AND PROGRESSING MIND

19: THE TEMPLE OF THE LIVING GOD

20: I AM OK

21: THE SPIRIT OF TRUTH

22: THE PERFECT PERMANENCY

23: THE FATHER GOD, GOD, GOD THE FATHER

24: HUSBAND, WIFE AND CHILD

25: GOD AND HIS HARBINGER

26: LIFE EVERLASTING

27: POSSESS

28: MY MIND AND MY PLAN

29: AFTER HEART AND AFTER MIND

30: MY DECLARATION & STAND IN BCS

31: BEYOND THE HOPE OF FAITH

32: MENTAL STAIN

33: THE PRINCIPLE OF SELF HOLD

34: THE MASTERSHIP

35: HIDU-CUM

36: THE UNIVERSAL PARENT

37: ADVANCED YOU AND ME

38: THE GREAT UNIVERSAL CHANGE

39: THE PROJECTED MIND
40: INDESTRUCTIBLE BLESSED FIVE STARS

41: ASTROTS, GOD PRESENT I AND MY FATHER

42: SONGS THE COMPLETION

43: THE RIGHT BUTTON

44: AKWA ABASI IBOM- ETE - DIRECTING NDITO AKWA IBOM

45: THE DIGITAL AGE

46: GOD IS OFFICIAL CHAMPION

47: A TRUE WITNESS

48: MYSTERY OF PROCREATION AND BIRTH

49: THE UNIVERSAL UMBRELLA

50: THE FORERUNNER

51: A OF A TO Z (FIRST OF ALL)

52: MAN IN THREE CAPACITIES

53: THE TRUE LIFE OF HOLY SPIRIT PERSONIFIED

54: IN-BETWEEN THE FATHER & THE SON

55: DIVINE ARRANGEMENT & AUTHORITY

56: TWENTY FIRST CENTURY IS NOT FOR SATAN

57: THE SUPREME WORD SEASON CELEBRATION

58: THE MAXIMUM DEITY

59: TRANSFORMER TRANSMITTER AND WAVE

60: THE SUPREME FUTURE

61: THE BYLOVE OF WORD

62: <u>THE SIGNATURE OF THE FATHER GOD</u>

63: THE TWO WAYS

64: THE UNDERSTANDING OF LIFE

65: THE GREATER THAN SOLOMON IS HERE

66: <u>THE CONQUEROR</u>

67: THE SPIRITUAL GENERAL INSPECTOR OF LIFE

68: THE NIGERIA IN THE AFRICA Part one

69: THE NIGERIA IN THE AFRICA Part two

70: THE CREATOR AND CREATIONS PART ONE

71: THE CREATOR AND CREATIONS PART TWO

72: THE CREATOR AND CREATIONS PART THREE

73: THE SUPREME TEACHER

74: THE SPIRITUAL COVER

75: THE NIGERIA IN THE AFRICA PART THREE

76: THE SUPREME BELIEVE

77: CAST AND BAN (LECTURE IN LIVERPOOL)

78: LIFE EXTENSION MANUAL

79: THE SPIRITUAL TRAFFIC

80: THE VOICE OF THE CREATOR

81: MY OFFICE

82: LIFE SPIRITUAL FIRE EXTINGUISHER

83: INFORMATION

84: FATHER GOD FINAL ARRANGEMENT

85: THE LOVERS OF CHRIST

86: I LOVE YOU, I LOVE YOU TOO

87: THE UNIVERSAL SUPREME UPDATE

88: THE SUPREME ALTAR

89: THE SOURCE AND DESTINATION

90: A SON LIKE THE FATHER THE KING OF KINGS A ROOTS FROM HEAVEN (NOT THIS TIME AROUND)

91: THE TRUE WITNESS AND THE TRUE SERVANT

92: THE FINAL ARRANGEMENT

93: A TRUE NIGERIAN MAN AND WOMAN

94: EVERYONE MUST PERSONALLY INVOLVE

95: BEWARE

96: ESIEN EMANA AKPAN "THE AFRICAN PROBLEMS"

97: THE SECRET OF THE UNIVERSAL PROBLEMS AND THE REMEDY (MUSLIM AND CHRISTIAN FROM THE SAME PARENT)

98: MMU-UDIM – THE BLESSED MOTHER (ABASI ME UDIM)

99: THINK WELL, SPEAK WELL AND DO WELL

100: THE STAGES OF HOW TO PROCESS THE WORD

101: EVIL STAIN, WHO RUNS AWAY FROM WHO

102: BEYOND HUMAN KNOW PURELY SPIRITUAL

103: <u>THE INSPIRATIONAL WRITER</u>

104: BIAKPAN OBIO AKPAN ABASI (THE NEW JERUSALEM CITY)

105: "OBAMA" THE STRAINTHEN AND THE SPIRIT OF BILL GATE AND MICROSOFT

106: THE HOLY TRINITY

107: AMEN –ODUWEM IKO ABASI

THANK YOU FATHER

www.ingramcontent.com/pod-product-compliance
Lightning Source LLC
Chambersburg PA
CBHW021810220426
43662CB00006B/249